Preface

Spotlight on History, Volume 1 is your new book for your bilingual history classes. You'll find the following elements in the book:

SOURCES are the key materials for your work. They are numbered throughout in each subchapter. There is also a short caption which explains the *Source*. *Sources* can be authentic documents like texts, drawings, photographs, or they can be adapted materials like simplified texts, sketches, diagrams, maps or statistics.

TASKS tell you how to use the *Sources*. Like the *Sources* they are numbered and they have a thematic title for easy reference. By following the tasks you will cover all the *Sources*. *Tasks* printed in blue are addressed to learners with a special interest in this area. Sometimes they are more difficult than the other tasks, and in other cases they take a bit longer or are based on group work.

The FEATHER SYMBOL tells you that this is a writing task.

The BOOK SYMBOL tells you that you should do some extra research. This could be in your German/English history book, in an encyclopedia or any other reference material that is available to you.

The BIG QUOTATION MARKS at the end of a task refer to additional vocabulary which appears under the same symbol on the left or right of a double page. This will help you to do the task. The headlines give you extra information about specific themes like "technological problems", or particular skills like "describing photographs".

The ARROW in a task refers to the *Glossary* (p. 91) or to the *Biographies* (p. 95). Both are arranged in alphabetical order and give you background information on specific themes, problems or historical figures.

The THREE TRIANGLES give you the new vocabulary of the different *Sources* and *Tasks* of each double page. Look for the symbols which are always on the far right or left side of the page. Under the symbol you'll find the number of the *Source* and definitions or translations of the new words. If you need the exact German translation, you can look it up in the English-German *Vocabulary* (p. 99) or in the German-English *Historical Dictionary* (p. 108).

HISTORY SKILLS-boxes help you to analyse the *Sources* which require certain skills, e.g. analysing a cartoon or explaining a diagram.

The TIME LINE on p. 86 gives you an overview of the three chapters (The American Revolution, the Industrial Revolution, Imperialism). It gives you the most important dates and events for each chapter and also shows how each chapter is linked to the other two.

The EXTRA READING LIST on p. 90 is a list of books and reference works which you can read or use when you are particularly interested in a subject from *Spotlight on History, Volume 1*. The *Reading List* gives you short summaries of the books and the order number. The colour dot (● ● ●) tells you which chapter the book belongs to.

We hope that you'll enjoy working with *Spotlight on History, Volume 1*.

The American Revolution

1 Introduction: Linking the present and the past

1.1 Advertisements: Using or misusing history?

SOURCE 1

1.2 Flags: Belonging, but where?

SOURCE 2: American schoolchildren saluting the flag

The Pledge of Allegiance

I pledge allegiance to the flag of the United States of America and to the republic for which it stands, one nation under God, indivisible, with liberty and justice for all.

SOURCE 3

Explain the clues in the advertisement (Source 1):
1 the girl[1], the torch in her right hand, the date (③)
2 the boy[2], the stripes on his hat and trousers (①), the stars on his hat (②).
(You may want to look up the following in the glossary: [1] Statue of Liberty, p. 94; [2] Uncle Sam, p. 95.)

1.3 Coins: Recalling values

SOURCE 5

Give your opinion:
"Using national symbols in an advertisement – a misuse?"

Discuss what your reaction would be if you were asked to salute the German flag at school every morning. (Note where the children in *Source 2* have their hands.)

Explain and compare (*Source 4*):
1 Name the two flags that are national flags today.
2 Four flags have stripes and two also have stars. Count them and explain.
3 Look at flag C and explain the details:
  a Why was a snake chosen?
  b What does the slogan mean?
  c Who should not tread on whom?
4 Put flags A to E in the order in which they may have been used. Give reasons for the order you have chosen.

Explain (*Source 5*) the meaning behind:
1 the portrait of George Washington (→ p. 95) on the coin (①)
2 "LIBERTY" (②)
3 "IN GOD WE TRUST" (③)
4 "E PLURIBUS UNUM" (④), a Latin phrase meaning "one out of many"
5 the eagle (⑤).

Source 2
• *(to) salute sb./sth.* greet sb./sth. formally

Source 3
• *pledge* [pledʒ] formal promise
• *allegiance* [əˈliːdʒəns] support or loyalty, e.g. towards a nation or a leader
• *indivisible* [ˌɪndɪˈvɪzəbl] sth. that cannot be divided (unteilbar)
• *liberty* freedom, especially in political and religious questions
• *justice* [ˈdʒʌstɪs] fairness; equal chances or opportunities

Source 4
• *(to) tread on sb./sth., trod, trodden* [tred, trɒd, ˈtrɒdn] step on sb./sth.

SOURCE 4

2 Colonizing the New World

2.1 Emigrating to the New World

SOURCE 1: A man called James Oglethorpe wrote the passage on the right in order to raise the money that he needed to take the first group of settlers to Georgia.

Such a colony will feed many families who are presently suffering from hunger, as well as making them masters of houses and lands. This will take the pressure off those people in Great Britain who, at the moment, have to support these poor families. Numbers of [British] manufacturers will produce clothes, working tools and other things that are needed by the colonists. …

The colony of Georgia lies about as far south as parts of China, Persia, Palestine, and the Madeiras. So it is highly probable that when Georgia is well peopled and rightly cultivated, England may import silk, wine, oil, dyes, drugs and many other materials for manufacture from there. These products must now be bought from southern countries.

Reasons for emigration in the 17th and 18th centuries:
1. According to *Source 1*, what made Georgia attractive to *different* people in Britain?
2. Give a first impression of *Source 2* using clues ① – ④. Then study the entry on "Puritans" in the glossary (p. 92) and comment on the scene in the picture.

SOURCE 2: Leaving home

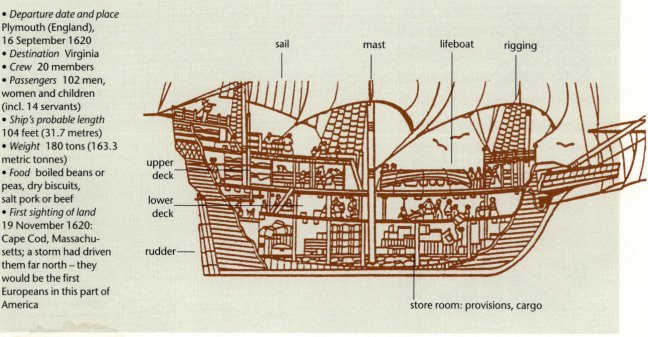

- *Departure date and place* Plymouth (England), 16 September 1620
- *Destination* Virginia
- *Crew* 20 members
- *Passengers* 102 men, women and children (incl. 14 servants)
- *Ship's probable length* 104 feet (31.7 metres)
- *Weight* 180 tons (163.3 metric tonnes)
- *Food* boiled beans or peas, dry biscuits, salt pork or beef
- *First sighting of land* 19 November 1620: Cape Cod, Massachusetts; a storm had driven them far north – they would be the first Europeans in this part of America

SOURCE 3: The Mayflower

The American Revolution 5

① **Familiar items**
Collect all the words you understand and group them under the following headings: food, clothes, tools.
(Where necessary, check the modern spelling. Don't be worried about the unusual printing:
ſ, s = s
§ = Poorer people did not have to take items marked with this symbol.)

② **Weights and measures**
These can be difficult to understand once you are outside the modern metric system. Transfer the weights and measures in the text into metric specifications.
- *hogshead* large container holding 63 gallons (German: "Oxhoft"; cf. "hog": male pig)
- *hundred weight* 1/20 of one ton; 100 pounds (US)
- *bushell* = bushel 8 gallons
- *gallon* 4 quarts
- *quart* 2 pints
(1 pint = 0.57 litres)
- *dozen* twelve

SOURCE 4: This is a list of some of the things which a settler family was advised to take to America. It was printed in 1630.

> Victuall.
> Aleale, one Hogshead.
> Malt, one Hogshead.
> Beefe, one hundred waight.
> Porke pickled, 100. or Bacon 74. pound.
> Pease, two bushells.
> Greates, one bushell.
> Butter, two dozen.
> Cheese, halfe a hundred.
> Vineger, two gallons.
> § Aquavita, one gallon.
> Mustard seed, two quarts.
> § Salt to save Fish, halfe a hogshead.
>
> Apparell.
> Shooes, six payre.
> § Boots for men, one payre.
> Leather to mend shooes, foure pound.
> Irish stockings, foure payre.
> Shirts, six.
> Handkerchiefes twelve.
> One Sea Cape or Gowne, of course cloth.
> Other apparell, as their purses will afford.
>
> Tooles which may also serve a family of foure or five persons.
> One English Spade.
> One steele Shovell.
> Two Hatchets.
> Axes 3. one broad axe, and 2. felling axes.
> One Wood hooke.
> Howes 3. one broad of nine inches, and two narrow of five or six inches.
> One Wimble, with sixe piercer bits.
> One Hammer.
> Other tooles as mens severall occupations require, as Hand sawes

③ **Intelligent guessing**
Try to think of words in German or another language you know that are like the unfamiliar words:
malt   Malz
meale   Mehl
Aquavita ?

Think logically about the context:

↗ to save ↖
salt   ?   fish

④ **Annotations**
If you cannot work out the meanings of all the words and feel you cannot do without them, the annotations below will help you.

▼▼▼

Source 1
- *silk* smooth, fine cloth (Seide)
- *dye* [daɪ] substance used to change the colour of cloth, hair etc. (Färbemittel)

Source 2
- *(to) be burnt at the stake* be tied to a post made of wood before being burnt to death (auf dem Scheiterhaufen sterben)

Source 4
- *victuall* = *victuals* ['vɪtlz] food and drink
- *pickle* salt-water or vinegar (cf. below) for keeping meat and vegetables for a long time
- *pea* small round green vegetable (Erbse)
- *greates* = *grits* Grütze
- *vinegar* ['vɪnɪgə] sharp-tasting liquid made from wine, used for salad dressing
- *mustard seed* ['mʌstəd] Senfkörner
- *stocking* one of a pair of pieces of clothing worn on the feet and legs
- *course cloth* = *coarse cloth* [kɔːs] cloth made for sails
- *hatchet* light, short-handled axe
- *howe* = *hoe* ['həʊ] long-handled garden tool used for turning the soil
- *wimble, piercer bit* ['pɪəsə] tools for boring holes
- *occupation* job
- *(to) require sth.* need sth.

The "Pilgrims" and the Mayflower
(Source 3):
1. Look up "Pilgrims" in the glossary (p. 94) to find out more about the people aboard the ship.
2. Imagine that it is 1620 and you are aboard the Mayflower making the crossing to North America. Use the information given (and your imagination) to write two to three diary entries about the crossing, problems on board, your hopes and worries. Begin with 17 September. Try to be accurate and think carefully about what Puritans at the time might have thought about.

Packing for a new life – Developing reading skills (Source 4):
1. Follow steps ① – ④ to understand the text.
2. What does the list tell you about the future life of the settlers?
3. If you wanted to emigrate and were able to take only five items, what would you take?

2.2 The colonies

SOURCE 5: Puritans on their way to church in the 17th century

① clout (piece of cloth; scarf)
② clog (wooden-soled shoe)
③ cloak (overcoat without sleeves)
④ breeches ['brɪtʃɪz] (short trousers fastened below the knee)

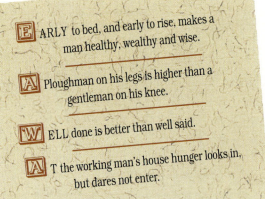

EARLY to bed, and early to rise, makes a man healthy, wealthy and wise.

A Ploughman on his legs is higher than a gentleman on his knee.

WELL done is better than well said.

AT the working man's house hunger looks in, but dares not enter.

SOURCE 6: Epigrams from Benjamin Franklin's "Poor Richard's Almanac" (1732–1757) (→)

SOURCE 7: "Penn's Peace Treaty with the Indians" (1771) by Benjamin West

▼▼▼

Source 6
- *epigram* short saying which expresses an idea in a clever and amusing way
- *almanac* ['ɔːlmənæk] calendar
- *wealthy* ['welθi] rich
- *(to) dare* be brave enough to do sth. dangerous without fear (etwas wagen)
- *ploughman* ['plaʊmən] person who ploughs (turns over) the soil
- *(to) keep sth. in fuel* keep sth. burning
- *learned* ['lɜːnɪd] having a lot of knowledge through studying

Life in the colonies:

1. Give a first impression of what *Sources 5–7* tell you about everyday life in the colonies.
2. Describe the people in *Source 5*: Consider their clothes, outward appearance and gestures.
   a. Explain why they may be walking in this order.
   b. What may the two men at the front be talking about?
3. Explain the different sayings in *Source 6*. What do they tell you about the way the settlers thought, felt and behaved?
4. "Walk through" *Source 7* from left to right and from the foreground to the background. Describe what you can see and find out what is going on in this scene.
5. Compare the relationship between the early settlers and the Native Americans as shown in *Source 7* with what you know about their later history.

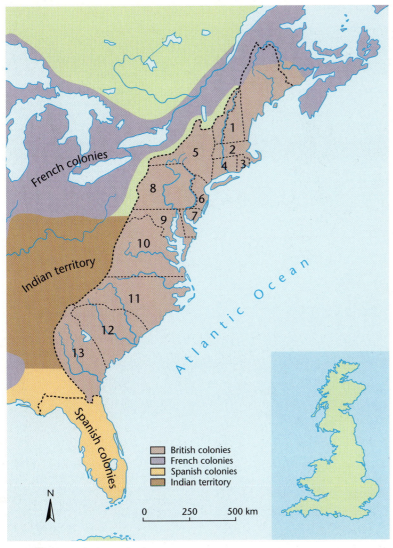

SOURCE 8: The thirteen colonies

The founding of the British colonies in America
Virginia (1607)
Massachusetts (1620)
New Hampshire (1623)
New York (1624, Dutch Colony from 1624–1625)
New Jersey (1629, Dutch and Swedish Colony from 1629–1664)
Maryland (1634)
Connecticut (1635)
Rhode Island (1636)
Delaware (1638)
North Carolina (1653)
South Carolina (1670)
Pennsylvania (1682)
Georgia (1733)

Year	Total
1660	75,000
1680	151,500
1700	250,900
1720	466,200
1740	905,600
1760	1,593,600
1780	2,780,400

SOURCE 9: Estimated colonial population

Maps and statistics in history:
1. Compare the map *(Source 8)* with a present-day map of the USA.
   a Name the thirteen colonies according to their numbers. Name the capitals and other important cities of the former colonies. Find the thirteen colonies on the present-day map.
   b Measure the distance between Massachusetts and Georgia. What city or town is about the same distance from your hometown?
2. Use the phrases in "Speaking about statistics" to describe the population trend between 1660 and 1780 *(Source 9)*.
3. Relate *Source 9* to *Sources 7 and 8:* What is likely to happen to the settlers in the colonies as more and more people pour into the country? Consider land, Native Americans ("Indians") and other colonies.

HISTORY SKILLS

Speaking about statistics

 Figures are | increasing / rising / climbing / going up | sharply / dramatically. / slightly / gradually. / by | … per cent. / 1.2 million.
There is an increase/rise in …

 Figures are | decreasing. / falling.
There is a decrease/drop in …

→ Figures remain steady.

2.3 Britain as a colonial power

SOURCE 10: Colonial products, 1696–1774

The southern colonies
In the southern colonies the climate and the soil were ideal for plantation agriculture. Crops such as cotton, tobacco and rice were grown on large plantations. Towards the end of the 17th century black slaves were shipped from Africa to work on these plantations in large numbers.

For the American plantation owners the slaves meant cheap labour. For British merchants the American plantations created the chance to follow a triangular route between Great Britain, Africa and the thirteen colonies in America.

> **Some colonial economic terms**
> Here are some economic words and phrases important to understanding the many quarrels between England and the colonies.
>
> **agrarian** [ə'greəriən] agricultural or farm economy
> **finished products** manufactured goods
> **exports** goods sold to another country
> **import** goods bought from another country
> **industrialized** having factories for manufacturing finished products
> **mercantilism** ['mɜːkəntɪlɪzm] economic system in which nations tried to export more than they imported. It developed in Europe after 1500. Colonies and trade monopolies were important parts of mercantilism.
> **monopoly** [mə'nɒpəli] complete control of a product by a single company, group, or nation
> **raw materials** [rɔː] natural substances that are used in manufacturing goods
> **resources** [rɪ'sɔːsɪz] minerals, soil, forests, water and energy sources
> **(to) trade** exchange, buy or sell goods (also: the trade of/in …)
> **balance of trade:**
> **favourable** ~ more exports than imports;
> **unfavourable** ~ more imports than exports

	Export	Import
New England	45,000	250,000
New York	60,000	285,000
Pennsylvania	40,000	210,000
Virginia + Maryland	415,000	420,000
Carolina	180,000	200,000
Georgia	6,000	23,000

SOURCE 11: Trade between the American colonies and England, 1762 (in pounds sterling)

1651	Navigation Acts: All goods shipped to England and its colonies had to be transported on British ships only.
1660	Colonies were allowed to export tobacco, wool, silk, sugar and indigo to England only.
1699	Colonies were no longer allowed to export wool.
1732	Colonies were forbidden to export hats to England or Europe.
1750	Colonies were no longer allowed to produce ironware etc.

SOURCE 12: Acts of Parliament that affected the colonies

Relating history and economy:
1. Link up *Sources 10* and *11*: Explain the difference in the balance of trade between the northern and southern colonies.
2. Look at *Source 12*. Why do you think the British government passed those Acts of Parliament? The words on the left will help you.
3. Link up *Sources 11* and *12*: Describe the effects of the British acts on the different colonies in *Source 11*.
4. Copy the diagram of the triangular trade route into your exercise book. Then complete it to show the direction of the following goods: silk, rice, indigo, tobacco, slaves, tools, furs, iron ore, timber, alcohol, guns.

The American Revolution

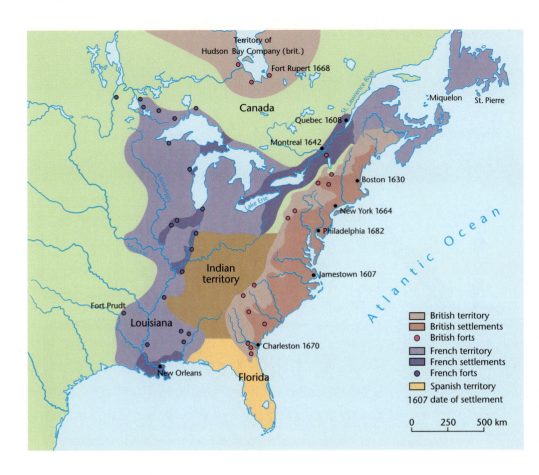

SOURCE 13: The European powers in North America

① Note the location of settlements.
② Note the size of the territories and actually settled parts.
③ Note the locations of the forts. Why were they built where they were?
④ Where could each of the powers expand to? Who was threatened by these possibilities?

▼▼▼

Source 10
- *fur* [fɜː] soft thick hair on the skin of animals
- *timber* wood prepared for use in building
- *triangular* [traɪˈæŋɡjʊlə] shaped like a triangle

Source 12
- *act* law made by parliament
- *navigation* travel on water
- *indigo* [ˈɪndɪɡəʊ] plant product used to give a deep blue colour to cloth
- *ironware* things made of iron

- *ore* Erz

Defending the colonies:

1. Look at the map *(Source 13)* closely.
   a Relate language and geography: Identify English- and French-sounding place names.
   b Relate past and present: What are the official languages of Canada today? Explain.
2. Use the clues in *Source 13* to explain the conflict of interest between France and Great Britain.
3. In 1763 France as a colonial power disappeared from the map of North America (→ "French and Indian War" p. 92). Explain the consequences for Great Britain and its colonies in North America.
4. Continue the dialogue below between a British officer (BO) and an American colonist (AC), in which they quarrel about the question of who has to pay. The arguments in the money bag will help you.
   - BO: It's about time you made a contribution to what we have done and indeed are still doing for you here in America.
   - AC: I don't see what you mean.
   - BO: Well, we fought for you, didn't we?
   - AC: That may be so, but …

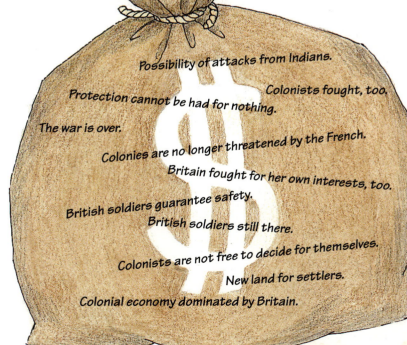

Possibility of attacks from Indians.
Colonists fought, too.
Protection cannot be had for nothing.
The war is over.
Colonies are no longer threatened by the French.
Britain fought for her own interests, too.
British soldiers guarantee safety.
British soldiers still there.
Colonists are not free to decide for themselves.
New land for settlers.
Colonial economy dominated by Britain.

3 From colonialism to independence

3.1 Taxation and opposition

SOURCE 1: A colonial newspaper reacts to the Stamp Act

The fatal stamp:
1. What does the headline of the *Pennsylvania Journal* (Source 1) say? Use your own words.
2. Explain the symbols that are used in *Source 1*.
3. Why does the *Pennsylvania Journal* (→) have to expire? Use the information in *Source 2* and link up clues ① and ②.
4. Taxation then and now:
   a What types of taxes do you know?
   b Imagine the tax on petrol is raised again. How do people react?

▼▼▼

Source 1
- *(to) expire* [ɪkˈspaɪə] come to an end; die
- *resurrection* [ˌrezəˈrekʃn] coming or bringing back to life again
- *dreadful* [ˈdredfl] unpleasant
- *dismal* [ˈdɪzməl] sad, miserable
- *doleful* sad, depressed
- *dolorous* [ˈdɒlərəs] sorrowful (schmerzlich)

Under the 1765 Stamp Act, taxes had to be paid for printed material of all kinds, like college diplomas and legal documents, but also for playing cards and dice.

The editors of newspapers, for example, had to pay a duty of one penny for every copy and two shillings for each advertisement. All such documents and materials had to bear a government stamp showing that the tax had been paid.

SOURCE 2: The Stamp Act (1765)

SOURCE 3: A handbill

WILLIAM JACKSON,

an IMPORTER; at the

BRAZEN HEAD,

North Side of the TOWN-HOUSE,

and Opposite the Town-Pump, in

Corn-hill, BOSTON.

It is desired that the SONS and DAUGHTERS of *LIBERTY*, would not buy any one thing of him, for in so doing they will bring Disgrace upon *themselves*, and their *Posterity*, for *ever* and *ever*, AMEN.

Colonial opposition:

1. Read and discuss *Sources 3 and 4*.
   a Divide the different means of opposition up into violent and non-violent, legal and illegal actions. The words on the right may help you.
   b Discuss what steps might have been most effective in the colonists' fight against the Stamp Act.
2. Study *Sources 3 and 4* and decide which of the different means of opposition they reflect.
3. What development do you see in the actions of the crowds in *Source 4*? (Clues ① – ④ will help you to follow the sequence of events.)

> **assassination**
> [əˌsæsɪˈneɪʃn]
> • (to) carry out an ~
> • (to) be the victim of an ~
> • an attempted ~
> • (to) assassinate sb.
> **boycott** [ˈbɔɪkɒt]
> • (to) impose / lift a ~
> • an economic / a trade ~
> • (to) boycott sb./sth.
> **demonstration**
> • a mass / spontaneous / an organized ~
> • (to) organize a ~
> • (to) demonstrate for / against sth.
> **hunger strike**
> • (to) be on a ~ ~
> • (to) go on a ~ ~
> **march**
> • a peaceful ~
> • a protest ~
> • (to) march for / against sth.
> **military action**
> [ˈmɪlɪtəri]
> • (to) conduct a ~ ~ against sb./sth.
> **riot** [ˈraɪət]
> • a ~ breaks out
> • (to) put down a ~
> • (to) riot
> **strike**
> • (to) be on ~
> • (to) go on ~

Yesterday morning at break of day was discovered hanging upon a tree in a street of the town an effigy, with inscriptions, shewing it was intended to represent Mr Oliver, the Secretary, who had lately accepted the office of Stamp distributor. Some of the neighbours offered to take it down, but they were given to know that would not be permitted. …

It grew dark when the mob, which had been gathering all the afternoon, came down to the Town House, bringing the effigy with them. … From thence they went to a new building, lately built by Mr Oliver to let out for shops, and not quite finished: this they called the Stamp Office, and pulled it down to the ground in five minutes. From thence they went to Mr Oliver's house, before which they beheaded the effigy; and broke all the windows next the street; then they carried the effigy to Fort Hill near Mr Oliver's house where they burnt the effigy in a bonfire. … The mob … beat in all the doors and windows of the garden front and entered the house. … As soon as they had got possession, they searched about for Mr Oliver, declaring they would kill him.

② time
③ place
④ action

SOURCE 4: The British governor reports on events in Boston. The Andrew Oliver mentioned in the report was a royal stamp-master.

▼▼▼

Source 3
• *(to) desire sth.* wish sth. strongly
• *disgrace* loss of respect
• *posterity* [pɒˈsterəti] future generations

Source 4
• *effigy* [ˈefɪdʒi] portrait or image of a person in stone, wood etc.
• *mob* large, noisy crowd of people
• *lately* not long ago
• *stamp distributor* [dɪˈstrɪbjutə] stamp-master
• *(to) permit sth.* allow sth.
• *(to) gather* meet
• *thence* (from) there
• *(to) behead sb.* cut off sb.'s head

Q: What is your name, and where are you from?
A: Franklin, from Philadelphia.
Q: Do you think it right that America should be protected by Great Britain and not pay any part of the expense?
A: That is not the case. During the French and Indian War, the colonies raised, clothed, and paid nearly 25,000 troops and spent many millions of dollars of their own. ...
Q: Was it an opinion in America before 1763 that the British Parliament had no right to tax Americans?
A: I never heard any objection to taxes on trade. But Parliament never had a right to set taxes within America, as we are not represented in Parliament. ...
Q: What do you think the consequences will be if the Stamp Act is not repealed?
A: A total loss of respect and affection for Great Britain, and of the commerce that depends on that respect and affection. ...
Q: If the act is repealed, will the colonists acknowledge the right of Parliament to tax them? Will they repeal their resolutions against the Stamp Act?
A: No, never.
Q: Can anything force the colonists to repeal the resolutions?
A: No power, however great, can force people to change their opinions.

SOURCE 5: In 1766 Benjamin Franklin (→) appeared before Parliament in London as a representative of the colonies. This passage was adapted from his testimony.

① capital letters (North Carolina)

② snake: symbolic meaning?

③ slogan

SOURCE 6: Cartoon by Benjamin Franklin (1765)

Source 5
- *expense* cost
- *objection to sth.* arguments against sth.
- *affection* love
- *commerce* trade
- *(to) acknowledge sth.* [əkˈnɒlɪdʒ] etwas anerkennen
- *(to) repeal sth.* take sth. back officially
- *resolution* formal decision taken at a meeting
- *testimony* [ˈtestɪmənɪ] written or spoken statement declaring that sth. is true

Organizing resistance:
1. Sum up the British arguments for and the American arguments against the Stamp Act (*Source 5*).
2. The colonists used the slogan "no taxation without representation". Use Franklin's answer to explain what they meant by that.
3. Try to explain why the colonists' reaction was so strong.
4. Describe the different elements of *Source 6* and explain its message. Use clues ① – ③.
5. An earlier version of the poster shown in *Source 6* was used to encourage unity among the colonies during the French and Indian War. Why, from the American point of view, was unity just as important in 1765?

The British had spent a lot of money in their wars against France. By 1763 the government had a national debt of £138 million. Part of that money had been spent defending the colonists against the French. Some British politicians felt it right that the colonists should pay towards their own defence in the future and meet the cost of the British army that was still stationed in the colonies.

1764	**Sugar Act** ① – angry reaction but no rebellion in the colonies	
1765	**Stamp Act** ② – widespread opposition: meeting of delegates from the different colonies in New York under the banner of "no taxation without representation"; protest meetings, riots, attacks against stamp-masters, boycott of British goods	
1766	**Stamp Act** – repealed **Declaratory Act** ③ – passed	
1767	**Townshend Duties** ④ – boycott of British goods organized by Assembly (state parliament) of Massachusetts; Massachusetts Assembly dismissed by British parliament; rioting against British property in Boston, Massachusetts	
1770	**Townshend Duties** – repealed, with the exception of the duty on tea	

① Sugar Act (→): increased the tax on all sugar imported into the colonies from West India

② Stamp Act (→): cf. p. 10

③ Declaratory Act (→): said that the British had the right to impose internal taxes on the colonies whenever they wanted to

④ Townshend Duties (→): import taxes on goods exported from Britain to the colonies like glass, paper, paint and tea

SOURCE 7: Taxation and opposition – a timetable

Determining cause-effect relationships *(Source 7)*:

1 Make a time-line of the events between 1764 and 1770 to illustrate the conflict of interests between Great Britain and her American colonies:

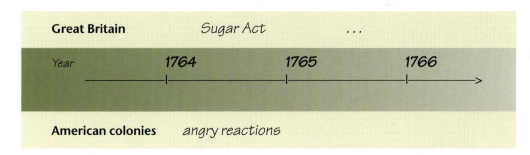

2 Choose a number of events that can be paired as **causes** and **effects**. Explain **why** things happened and **what consequences** they had. Then complete the following chart.

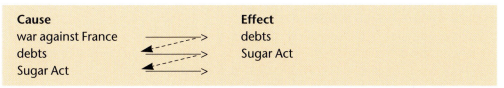

3 Use your chart as a basis for a detailed text about taxation and opposition between 1764 and 1770. The words on the right will help you.

Cause and effect
(to) **lead to** sth.
(to) **cause** sth.
(to) **bring** sth. **about**
(to) **provoke** sth.
(to) **produce** sth.
(to) **depend on** sth.
(to) **result in** sth.
(to) **originate from** sth.
(to) **give rise to** sth.
(to) **trigger** sth. **(off)**
(to) **follow from** sth.
(to) **be followed by** sth.
(to) **react by** doing sth.
(to) **respond to** sth.
because (of sth.)
as a result of sth.
at the root of sth.
the source of sth.
the reason why
as a consequence (of sth.)
the outcome of sth.
one result was …
(to) **have effects on** sth.
sb.'s **answer was** …
reaction to …

3.2 The Boston Massacre

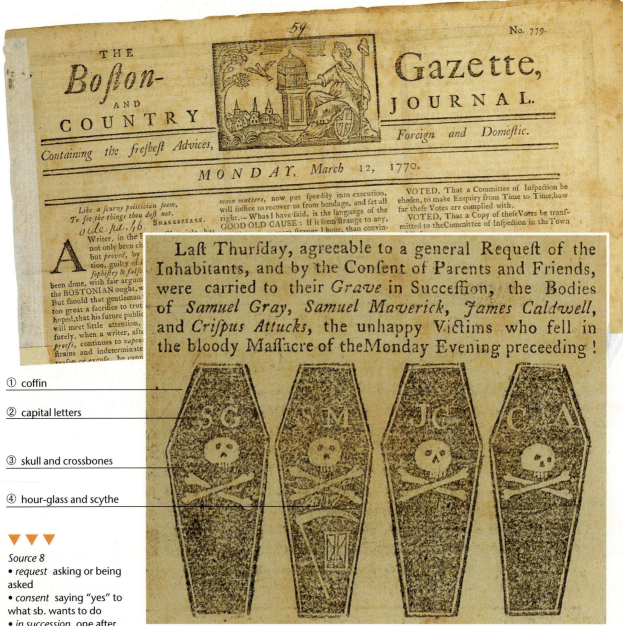

① coffin

② capital letters

③ skull and crossbones

④ hour-glass and scythe

SOURCE 8: Page of a Boston newspaper

▼▼▼

Source 8
• *request* asking or being asked
• *consent* saying "yes" to what sb. wants to do
• *in succession* one after the other
• *Monday preceding* last Monday
• *scythe* [saɪð] Sense

Source 10
• *(to) assemble* come together in a group
• *(to) insult sb.* hurt sb.'s feelings
• *sentry* guard
• *(to) strike sth.* hit sth.
• *rascal* [ˈrɑːskl] dishonest person
• *lobster, bloodyback* words for British soldiers, referring to their red uniforms (*lobster* = Hummer; *bloody* = blutig)
• *scoundrel* [ˈskaʊndrəl] bad person

Reconstructing the events of March 1770:

1. What does *Source 8* tell you about the events in Boston?
   a. Write two or three sentences which tell what the article is about.
   b. Describe and analyse the symbolical meanings of clues ① – ④.
2. Describe the events as they are shown in the illustration (*Source 9*).
   a. Who are the two groups of people? Who is the man on the far right?
   b. Which side do you think the artist is on? Give reasons for your opinion.
3. Read the eye-witness reports in *Source 10*.
   a. Put the different pieces of information together.
   b. How do you explain the different presentations of the events?

	engraving	witnesses Cain & Wyat	witness Preston
action leading to the event			
no. of people involved			
people's behaviour			
soldiers' behaviour			
Preston's role			

SOURCE 9: American illustration showing the events in Boston's King Street on 5 March 1770

a Thomas Cain, an eye-witness to the scene in King Street, reported:
Between 30 and 40 people, mostly youngsters and boys, assembled in front of the town hall and then they gave cheers and asked where the soldiers were. Some of the people insulted the sentry standing nearby at the Custom House door and I saw some snowballs and other things being thrown in his direction. As a result of this the sentry stepped on the Custom House steps, loaded his gun and hit the steps three or four times with its wooden end.

b Another observer, William Wyat, claimed that the officer of the day, Captain Preston …
… stepped behind the soldiers to the right. He ordered the soldiers to fire. When they did not do so, he stamped his foot on the ground and said, "Damn your bloods, fire, be the consequences what it will." Then the second man from the left fired off his gun and, after a very short pause, the others fired one after another as quickly as possible.

c Captain Preston himself reported that the townspeople …
… were striking their heavy sticks together and calling out, "Come on you rascals, you bloodybacks, you lobster scoundrels; fire if you dare, G-damn you, fire and be damned. We know you dare not."

He said that he had not ordered his soldiers to fire, but that he had gone …
… to that fatal place only to calm down the mob, help the sentry do his job and stop the soldiers from doing anything wrong by his presence. But the mob were violent and the soldiers, when they were insulted and attacked with the sticks, were provoked and so caused the tragic scene.

SOURCE 10: Eye-witness reports on the events in Boston

3.3 The crisis over tea

SOURCE 11: The Boston Tea Party, 16 December 1773

At ten o'clock in the morning on Thursday, 16 December 1773, the Old South Meeting House was crammed to the doors with 5,000 excited citizens. They were not there to hold a service. Instead they were discussing tea, and they were very angry. The tea in question was lying in three ships, the *Dartmouth*, the *Eleanor* and the *Beaver*, alongside Griffin's Wharf in the outer harbour. Each ship held more than 100 chests of tea – in all about 45,000 kg, worth more than £9,000. [...]

It was good tea. The people were angry because the British Parliament had put a tax on it. The tea merchants of Boston would have to pay a duty of 3 pence on every pound (450 g) before they could sell it to the public.

This duty annoyed the people of Boston. They believed that, as they had not elected any of the MPs, Parliament had no right to tax them. "No taxation without representation" was their motto. For years they had tried to persuade the British Government not to tax them, and eventually the British had lifted all their taxes – except the duty on tea.

"No" to the tea tax
The leaders of the citizens were determined not to pay the tea tax. So in the Meeting House, Sam Adams* was busy persuading his angry fellow citizens that the tea must be sent back to Britain. They agreed with him, and ordered Francis Rotch, the owner of the *Dartmouth*, to sail his ship with its cargo of tea back across the Atlantic.

Rotch refused. He said he did not dare leave harbour. He pointed out that according to the law, he ought to have paid the duty as soon as his ship entered port. If he tried to leave without paying, the British would certainly stop him. There were troops with cannons on Castle Island. They could easily stop his ship, or even sink it. Rotch said he would go if the governor, Thomas Hutchinson, gave him permission. Otherwise his ship would stay put.

Adams and his friends told Rotch to go to Governor Hutchinson and ask for permission to sail. This would take some time because the governor was at his country house at Milton, 11 km away. So the meeting broke up for a few hours while Rotch set off in pouring rain on his long ride. At three o'clock the men returned to the Meeting House.

Once again the hall was crowded. Most of those present were dressed as usual, but around the doors and in the gallery there were a few strange figures. They were obviously white men, but they had blackened their faces and wrapped blankets round their shoulders so that in the dark they could be mistaken for Indians. Inside the hall the speeches continued. Outside, the rain stopped, and it began to get dark. At a quarter to six there was a clatter of hooves. Rotch was back.

Rotch refuses to sail
Rotch made his way into the hall. It was now quite dark, except for pools of light here and there where a few candles had been lit. He made his report. The governor had refused to give him permission to sail, so his ship would stay where it was. Nobody was very surprised. They all knew that two of the governor's sons were tea merchants who would make a good profit if the tea was landed and sold.

There was a great shout from the crowd in the hall, and when order had been restored Sam Adams rose and said, "I do not see what else the inhabitants can do to save their country." His words must have been a signal, for they were at once answered by a war-hoop from one of the "Indians" in the gallery. This cry was repeated by those at the entrance. Others shouted, "Boston Harbour a teapot tonight" and "Hurrah for Griffin's Wharf!" as they ran out into the street shouting and screaming.

* Samuel Adams was the leader of the most extreme "patriots" in Massachusetts.

SOURCE 12: Excerpt from a British history textbook (1987)

⑧
tar¹ /tɑː(r)/ n [U] **1** thick black sticky liquid, hard when cold, obtained from coal, etc and used in making roads, to preserve timber, etc. **2** similar substance formed by burning tobacco: [attrib] *low-/middle-/high-tar cigarettes*.
▷ **tar** v (-rr-) **1** [Tn] cover (sth) with tar: *a tarred road, rope, roof*. Cf TARMAC. **2** (idm) **tar and 'feather sb** put tar on sb and then cover him with feathers, as a punishment. **tarred with the same 'brush (as sb)** having the same faults (as sb).
tar² /tɑː(r)/ n (also **Jack tar**) (*dated infml*) sailor.

SOURCE 13: *An English cartoon (1774)*

The Boston Tea Party – reconstructing the events:
1 Describe the scene in *Source 11*. Pay special attention to the people (①, ③), considering both how they are dressed and what they are doing.
2 Link up clues ② and ④ (*Source 11*) and speculate on what the people on the ship are throwing into the harbour and why the people in the foreground are cheering.
3 Make a table and fill in times and events mentioned in *Source 12*.

Time	Event
10 a.m.	...
11 a.m.	...

4 Go back to *Source 11* and finish the story that is told in *Source 12*.

Analysing a political cartoon (*Source 13*):
1 Describe the different objects and people. What are they doing?
   Who is the man in the centre, and what is happening to him (clues ④, ⑥, ⑧)?
2 Who are the other people in the foreground? Clue ② can help you to identify the group.
3 Identify symbols and read labels (clues ①, ②, ③, ⑤). Use your historical knowledge to explain their meaning.
4 Identify the artist's point of view. The combination of clues ① and ② and the faces of the men in the foreground will help you.
5 Do you agree or disagree with the "message" of the cartoonist?

HISTORY SKILLS

Political cartoons
A political cartoon is a drawing that presents an exaggerated point of view. Some cartoons express a positive point of view. More often, however, cartoons are critical of an event, person or group. Cartoons are powerful means of communication because they often present their message in a simple and direct manner. To get across this message, cartoonists often use symbolism, which is the use of one thing to stand for another. They may also use labels to help identify important symbols.

When analysing political cartoons, do what you have just done in the section "Analysing a political cartoon" (left):
– Describe figures and objects.
– Decide which objects are symbols.
– Read all labels.
– Identify the cartoonist's point of view: Determine whether the figures are presented in a positive or negative light. Are the figures or objects exaggerated in any way?

4 Winning independence

4.1 The Declaration of Independence

SOURCE 1

(335)
The PENNSYLVANIA EVENING POST

Vol. II.] Price only Two Coppers. Published every *Tuesday, Thursday,* and *Saturday* Evenings. [Num. 228.

SATURDAY, JULY 6, 1776.

In CONGRESS, July 4, 1776.
A Declaration by the Representatives of the United States of America, in General Congress assembled.

WHEN, in the course of human events, it becomes necessary for one people to dissolve the political bands which have connected them with another, and to assume, among the powers of the earth, the separate and equal station to which the laws of nature and of nature's God intitle them, a decent respect to the opinions of mankind requires that they should declare the causes which impel them to the separation.

We hold these truths to be self-evident, That all men are created equal; that they are endowed, by their Creator, with certain unalienable rights; That to secure these rights, and the pursuit of happiness. governments are instituted among men, deriving their just powers from the consent of the governed; that whenever any form of government becomes destructive of these ends, it is the right of the people to alter or to abolish it, and to institute new government, laying its foundation on such principles, and organizing its powers in such form, as to them shall seem most likely to effect their safety and happiness.

He has dissolved Representative Houses repeatedly, for opposing with manly firmness his invasions on the rights of the people.
He has refused for a long time, after such dissolutions, to cause others to be elected; whereby the legislative powers, incapable of annihilation, have returned to the people at large for their exercise; the state remaining in the mean time exposed to all the dangers of invasion from without, and convulsions wi[thin] ... the population of these
He has ... naturaliza-
states; for
tion of fo
migration
priations
He ha
his assen
He ha
tenure c
falaries.
He has erected a multitude of new
swarms of officers to harrass our p
substance.
He has kept among us,
without the consent of
He has

Th Jefferson (signature)

SOURCE 2

Henrich Millers 813 Stück.
Pennsylvanischer Staatsbote.

Diese Zeitung kommt alle Wochen zweymal heraus, nämlich Dienstags und Freytags, für Sechs Schillinge des Jahrs.
N.B. All ADVERTISEMENTS to be inserted in this Paper, or printed single by HENRY MILLER, Publisher hereof, are by him translated gratis.

Im Congreß, den 4ten July, 1776.
Eine Erklärung durch die Repräsentanten der Vereinigten Staaten von America, im General-Congreß versammlet.

Wenn es im Lauf menschlicher Begebenheiten für ein Volk nöthig wird die Politischen Bande, wodurch es mit einem andern verknüpft gewesen, zu trennen, und un...

Er hat Gesetzgebende Körper an ungewöhnlichen, unbequemen und von der Niederlage ihrer öffentlichen Archiven entfernten Plätzen zusammen berufen, zu dem einzigen Zweck, um sie so lan...

SOURCE 2: *In the 18th century, a total of 38 different German-language newspapers were already being published in Pennsylvania and the other colonies. Next to Christopher Saur, the most prominent German printer was Henry Miller, whose* Pennsylvanischer Staatsbote (→) *published a German translation of the Declaration of Independence on 9 July 1776.*

▼▼▼
Source 1
- (to) dissolve sth. [dɪˈzɒlv] cut sth.; put an end to sth.
- (to) assume a station take on a role
- (to) intitle = (to) entitle sb. to (do) sth. give sb. the right to (do) sth.
- (to) impel sb. to (do) sth. drive or force sb. into (doing) sth.
- self-evident clear, easy to understand
- endowed provided
- unalienable, also in-[ʌnˈeɪliənəbl, ɪn-] unable to be transferred to another person or taken away
- pursuit of happiness [pəˈsjuːt] Streben nach Glück
- (to) derive sth. get sth.
- (to) alter sth. change sth.
- (to) abolish sth. [əˈbɒlɪʃ] put an end to sth.

The American Revolution

Wenn es im Lauf menschlicher Begebenheiten für ein Volk nötig wird die Politischen Bande, wodurch es mit einem andern verknüpft gewesen, zu trennen, und unter den Mächten der Erden eine abgesonderte und gleiche Stelle einzunehmen, wozu selbiges die Gesetze der Natur und des Gottes der Natur berechtigen, so erfordern Anstand und Achtung für die Meinungen des menschlichen Geschlechts, dass es die Ursachen anzeige, wodurch es zur Trennung getrieben wird.

Wir halten diese Wahrheiten für ausgemacht, dass alle Menschen gleich erschaffen worden, dass sie von ihrem Schöpfer mit gewissen unveräußerlichen Rechten begabt worden, worunter sind Leben, Freiheit und das Bestreben nach Glückseligkeit. Dass zur Versicherung dieser Rechte Regierungen unter den Menschen eingeführt worden sind, welche ihre gerechte Gewalt von der Einwilligung derer, die regiert werden, herleiten; dass sobald einige Regierungsform diesen Endzwecken verderblich wird, es das Recht des Volkes ist sie zu verändern oder abzuschaffen, und eine neue Regierung einzusetzen, die auf solche Grundsätze gegründet, und deren Macht und Gewalt solchergestalt gebildet wird, als ihnen zur Erhaltung ihrer Sicherheit und Glückseligkeit am schicklichsten zu sein dünket.

SOURCE 3: *The translation of the Declaration of Independence from the* Pennsylvanischer Staatsbote *(Source 2) in modern printing*

Getting orientated:
1. The man whose signature you see next to *Source 1* was mainly responsible for writing the Declaration of Independence. Find out who the "man behind the words" was, then look for more information about him in the glossary (→ p. 96).
2. The cartoon *(Source 4)* introduces you to popular feelings of the time in Britain's colonies. Apply what you have learned about analysing political cartoons (cf. p. 17) and explain it.

Understanding the text *(Sources 1–3)*:
1. Read the German text *(Source 3)* and ask your teacher about any words you do not understand.
2. Write a summary in German. Use your own words. Concentrate on the highlighted words.
3. Write a summary in English. Use your own words. Go from the German text to the English version.

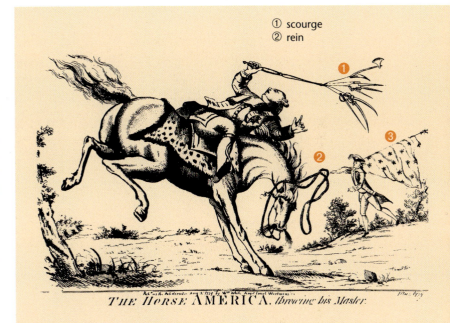

SOURCE 4: *"Throwing off an unwanted rider"* The cartoon was published in 1775. The man on horseback is King George III (→)

Working with the text:
1. The Declaration of Independence has been called "the birth-certificate of the USA". Copy three short passages from *Source 1* which justify this label.
2. When something new is born it replaces something old. Characterize the "old" in this instance (use *Source 4*).
3. Do your own research on German immigration to America and give a report in class. (You may find some helpful information in your German history book or your English textbook.)
4. Compare the first three lines of the second paragraph of the Declaration of Independence with Article 1 of the United Nations Declaration of Human Rights from 1948 *(Source 5)*. Point out similarities and differences.

Article 1
All human beings are born free and equal in dignity and rights. They are endowed with reason and conscience and should act towards one another in a spirit of brotherhood.

SOURCE 5: Excerpt from the United Nations Declaration of Human Rights

▼▼▼

Source 4
- *scourge* [skɜːdʒ] Geißel
- *rein* [reɪn] Zügel

Source 5
- *reason* Vernunft
- *conscience* [ˈkɒnʃəns] Gewissen

- *birth-certificate* document showing the date and place of a person's birth

① scourge
② rein

4.2 The Revolutionary War (1775–1783)

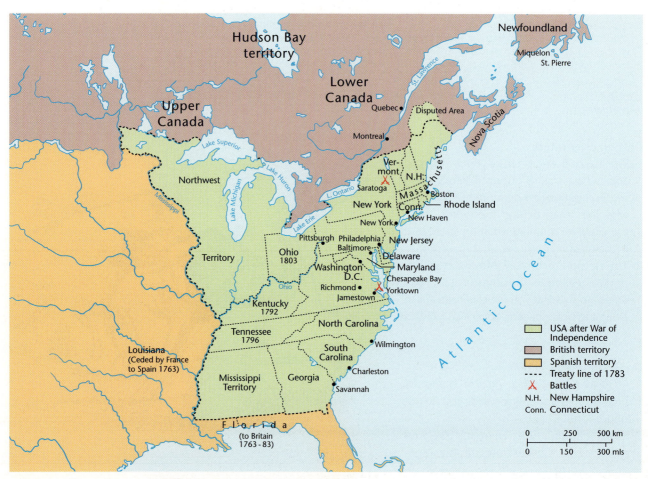

SOURCE 6: North America after the War of Independence

SOURCE 7: The Continental Navy Jack (1776)

Map skills – Locating places:
1. Find the place names mentioned in *Source 8* on the map *(Source 6)* and describe where they are located.

Fighting it out:
1. Put the paragraphs in *Source 8* into a logical order.
2. Explain in the given historical context what the flag *(Source 7)* wants to express (cf. symbol of the snake).
3. Compare the map *(Source 6)* with the one in *Source 13*, p. 9. Who has gained, who has lost territory?
4. After the Treaty of Paris, the Americans feared another war with Britain. Give reasons why. (Looking at the map in *Source 6* may help you.)

After reading each of the paragraphs, decide which sentence (A, B or C) best relates the main idea.

1. The battle of Saratoga in 1777 was an important turning point of the war for the American colonies. The English planned to divide the colonies in half by gaining control of the Hudson River Valley. The American victory at Saratoga stopped this plan. It showed the Americans that they might be able to win the war. The victory also impressed the king of France. After the battle, France joined the American side. France sent in needed supplies to the colonial army. French soldiers were sent in to fight against the English. The French navy also fought the English navy off the American coast.
   A. France signed a treaty to help England after the Battle of Saratoga.
   B. The Battle of Saratoga was an important American victory.
   C. England easily defeated America at the Battle of Saratoga.

2. When England signed the Treaty of Paris in 1783, the Revolutionary War was officially ended. England agreed that the United States was a free and independent country. Until then, England had felt that the American colonies were only part of the English empire in rebellion. In the treaty, England agreed to remove all its soldiers from the United States. Both sides agreed to free any prisoners captured during the war. England gave the United States full fishing rights off the Newfoundland coast. Most importantly, the Treaty of Paris set the boundaries of the United States. The boundaries were the Atlantic Ocean on the east, the Mississippi River on the west, the Great Lakes on the north, and Florida on the south.
   A. The Treaty of Paris ended the Revolutionary War with an English victory.
   B. After the Treaty of Paris, England still considered the United States part of its empire.
   C. When England signed the Treaty of Paris, it agreed that the United States was a free country.

3. American blacks fought on both the American and the English sides from the very beginning of the Revolutionary War. Within a year, however, slaves and free blacks were no longer allowed to join the American side. George Washington, general of the American army, was afraid that slave owners in the South would be angry if their slaves ran off to fight. Then England began recruiting blacks by promising them their freedom after the war was over. This persuaded the colonies to allow blacks to serve in the American army again.
   A. Blacks fought on both sides in the Revolutionary War.
   B. More blacks fought on the American side than on the English side.
   C. When the Revolutionary War began, most blacks fought for the English.

4. When the Revolutionary War broke out between England and the American colonies, England had many military advantages over the colonies. The English army was large and well trained. The American army was small and poorly organized. England had the most powerful navy in the world. The colonies had no navy at all when the war began. They had only privately owned ships, which had permission to attack the enemy. England had factories to make all the military supplies it needed. The colonies had few such supplies. England was also much better able to raise money to pay for the cost of the war than were the Americans.
   A. America's large army made it possible to win the Revolutionary War.
   B. The American army was larger and better trained than the English army.
   C. England had many military advantages over the colonies at the beginning of the war.

SOURCE 8: Extracts from an American history textbook. When reading this text, keep in mind that the paragraphs are in a jumbled order.

Source 8
• *supplies* [səˈplaɪz] arms and food
• *treaty* formal agreement between two countries
• *boundary* [ˈbaʊndri] line that marks a limit

5 Forming a nation

5.1 Creating a federal union

When America broke away from British rule in 1776, its leaders knew they would have to learn to rule themselves. The statements below describe the form of government between 1781 and 1788 in America.
- Many people in Virginia, the largest state, said: "We are Virginians first and Americans second."
- Each state had its own army; some even had a navy.
- Each state printed its own money.
- The neighbouring states taxed each other's goods.
- Some neighbouring states quarrelled over their frontiers.

FORMS OF GOVERNMENT

UNITARY

Under a unitary system, all major powers are located within the central government. State governments can act only by the rules or with the approval of the central government.

CONFEDERATION

In a confederation, independent states hold most of the major powers. In this system, state governments have protected their authority by creating and controlling a weak central government.

FEDERAL

A federal system of government divides power between a strong central government and the states. Certain powers are held by the central government, while others are held by the state governments. Some powers are shared. Both the central and the state governments have direct power over the people in certain areas.

SOURCE 1: Forms of government

▼▼▼

Source 1
- *unitary system* ['juːnɪtri] Zentral-, Einheitsstaat
- *confederation* Staatenbund
- *federal system* Bundesstaat
- *approval* [əˈpruːvl] Zustimmung

- *diversity* [daɪˈvɜːsəti] Vielfalt

Working with definitions:

1 Study the definitons in the box above and explain which form of government best describes the government in America between 1781 and 1786.

 2 Find out which form of government each of the following has. You may need to use an encyclopedia.
   a Community of Independent States (CIS)
   b Germany
   c European Union (EU)
   d Switzerland
   e France
   f United Kingdom

3 Give reasons why the Americans felt they needed to change their form of government after 1786.

5.2 Diversity and union

SOURCE 2: The Spirit of '76 (by Archibald M. Willard, 1836–1918)

SOURCE 3: A modern adaptation (TIME magazine)

The spirit of the USA:
1. Describe the people in the painting in *Source 2* (different groups, movements, looks, facial expressions).
2. The picture is called *The Spirit of '76*. Use your own words to describe what kind of "spirit" the artist wanted to express. Find adjectives to describe the three soldiers in the centre. – Point out details in the picture to explain how the artist tried to put this message across.
3. Identify the different people in *Source 3* (Native American, African American, white Anglo-Saxon, Hispanic, Asian).
   Explain why TIME magazine has changed some of the figures and what it wants to express in doing so.
4. From what you know about US history and society, how would you answer the TIME question: "Who are they?"

5.3 The Constitution

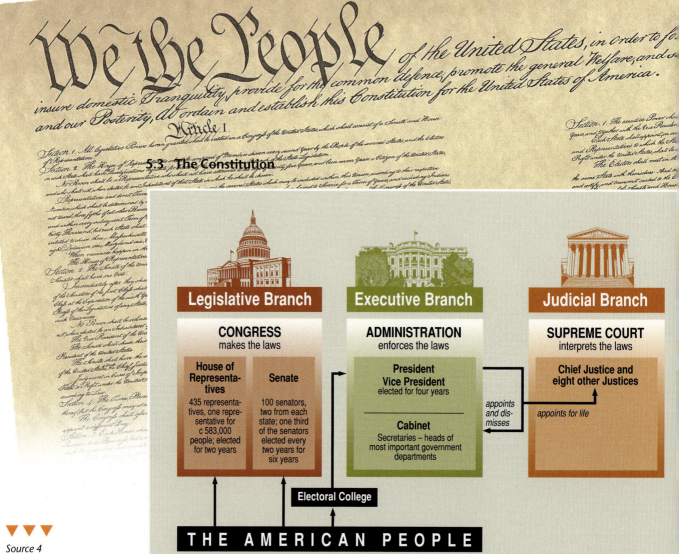

SOURCE 4: Who's who in American government

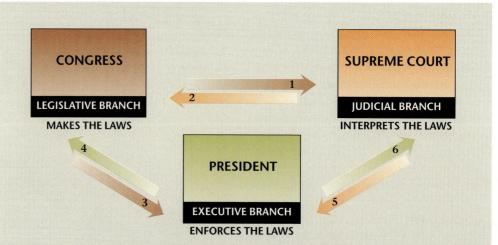

The makers of the Constitution made sure that each branch of government could control the other branches. For example the President can "check" Congress by vetoing, or rejecting laws it passes. On the other hand, Congress can remove the President if enough members feel that he or she has violated the law. Thus, both are kept in "balance".

SOURCE 5: Separation of Federal Powers: Examples of checks and balances

---

Source 4
- *legislative branch* ['ledʒɪslətɪv] gesetzgebende Gewalt
- *executive branch* [ɪɡ'zekjətɪv] vollziehende Gewalt
- *judicial branch* [dʒuː'dɪʃl] richterliche Gewalt
- *(to) enforce sth.* [ɪn'fɔːs] etwas Geltung verschaffen
- *administration* [əd,mɪnɪ'streɪʃn] Administration, Regierung
- *Cabinet* ['kæbɪnət] Kabinett
- *Justice* (AE) ['dʒʌstɪs] Richter/in am Obersten Gerichtshof
- *Chief Justice* (AE) Vorsitzende/r Richter/in am Obersten Gerichtshof
- *(to) appoint sb.* [ə'pɔɪnt] jn. ernennen
- *for life* auf Lebenszeit
- *dismiss sb.* [dɪs'mɪs] jn. entlassen

Source 5
- *(to) violate the law* commit a crime

The American Revolution

THE FEDERAL GOVERNMENT
has the power over matters that are important to the nation as a whole.
- National defense
- Foreign relations
- Foreign trade
- Trade among the states
- Money system
- Law enforcement (e.g. FBI)

EACH STATE GOVERNMENT
has power over most affairs within the state's borders.
- Health and safety
- Public building projects
- Education
- Highways
- Law enforcement (e.g. Highway Patrol)

EACH LOCAL GOVERNMENT
has power over the affairs of a county, city, or town.
- Parks
- Libraries
- Fire protection
- Streets and traffic
- Schools
- Water and sewage systems
- Law enforcement (e.g. sheriffs, police)

SOURCE 6: *The powers of each level of government in the American federal system*

SOURCE 7: *The Bill of Rights (1791; → p.90): The First Amendment*

CONGRESS shall make no law respecting an establishment of religion, or prohibiting the free exercise thereof; or abridging the freedom of speech, or of the press, or the right of the people peacefully to assemble and to petition the government for a redress of grievances.

Understanding American government
(Source 4):
1 Decide which of these statements are true and which are false.
   a The American people elect the President.
   b The Senate consists of 98 members.
   c There is one representative for 500,000 people.
   d The President appoints the Vice-President.
   e Senators are elected for two years.
   f The President dismisses the Justices.
   g In the USA government ministers are called "Secretaries".
   h The Administration is the Executive Branch.

Understanding checks and balances
(Source 5):
1 Match the numbers in the chart with the following:
   a can remove the President
   b appoints
   c can veto laws
   d can remove Justices
   e can declare laws unconstitutional
   f can declare actions by the President unconstitutional

Understanding federalism (Source 6):
1 Find out which level of government is responsible for performing the following services:
   a signing a peace treaty
   b setting limits on imported cars
   c hiring a schoolteacher

Understanding the Bill of Rights
(Source 7):
1 Copy the diagram below into your exercise-book and complete it.

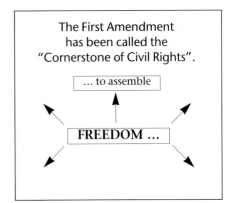

2 Discuss to what extent the makers of the Constitution learned from the past.

▼▼▼

Source 6
- *law enforcement* Durchführung der Gesetze
- *sewage* ['suːɪdʒ] Abwässer

Source 7
- *amendment* addition or change to a document
- *establishment* Einführung
- *(to) abridge sth.* [ə'brɪdʒ] limit sth.
- *(to) assemble* come together
- *(to) petition sb.* [pə'tɪʃn] ask sb. to do sth. one wants very much
- *redress* reparation for a wrong
- *grievance* ['griːvns] cause for complaint
- *unconstitutional* not in accordance with the constitution

5.4 Constitutions at work

SOURCE 8: Chicago artist Scott W. Tyler is arrested in October 1989 on the steps of the Capitol in Washington, D.C., after burning a US flag to protest against a law banning flag desecration.

In 1976, France and Britain wanted to land their new supersonic plane, called the Concorde, at American airports. Environmental groups in the USA opposed the idea.
President Ford's Secretary of Transportation decided that the Concorde could land at New York's Kennedy Airport. State government officials from New York and New Jersey run the airport. They refused to let the Concorde land at their airport.
The federal government took the states to court.

SOURCE 9: Case study: The Concorde dispute

Checks and balances in action:
1 Discuss *Source 8* in the context of the following information.
   a In 1989 the Supreme Court held that burning the American flag to express disagreement with governmental policies is a form of symbolic speech and therefore protected by the First Amendment.
   b Then President George Bush wanted an amendment to the Constitution that read: "The Congress and the States shall have power to prohibit the physical desecration of the flag of the United States."

Federalism in action (Source 9):
1 If you were a justice of the Supreme Court, how would you decide in the Concorde dispute?

▼▼▼

Source 8
• desecration [ˌdesɪˈkreɪʃn] Schändung, Entweihung

Source 9
• supersonic [ˌsuːpəˈsɒnɪk] having a speed greater than that of sound

• (to) prohibit sth. [prəˈhɪbɪt] forbid sth.

The German Constitution – A quiz

◆ What is the German constitution officially called?
   a Constitution of the Federal Republic of Germany
   b Basic Law ("Grundgesetz")
   c Treaty of Unification

◆ How is the president elected? – By …
   a the people
   b the parliament ("Bundestag")
   c by the Federal Assembly ("Bundesversammlung")

◆ For how many years is the president elected?
   a four
   b five
   c six

◆ How is the federal chancellor ("Bundeskanzler") elected? – By …
   a the people directly
   b the president
   c the parliament ("Bundestag")

◆ How can the Chancellor be forced to step down? – By …
   a the president
   b the constitutional court ("Bundesverfassungsgericht")
   c the parliament (vote of "no confidence")

◆ What is the German equivalent of the US senate?
   a the parliament
   b the constitutional court
   c the federal council ("Bundesrat")

◆ How many states ("Bundesländer") does the Federal Republic of Germany consist of since unification?
   a ten
   b fifteen
   c sixteen

◆ Who is the commander-in-chief of the armed forces ("Bundeswehr")?
   a the president
   b the chancellor
   c the minister of defense

◆ How can Germany's constitution be changed or amended? – By …
   a the people
   b the president
   c the parliament

6 "We the People …"

You have often read the term "We the People", but who could claim to belong to the American people? – The whites only – or the African and Native Americans, too?
Let's have a look at the changes since 1787.

SOURCE 1: 200 years after: Milestones

1789	white male property owners over 21 years of age (6% of adult male population)
1830	labourers, servants (male), immigrants
1870	former slaves
1920	women
1924	Native Americans
1971	all citizens 18 years of age or older

SOURCE 2: The right to vote in national elections

Fair shares for all?

1. Look at the people in *Source 1* and identify at least six of them. Use the information given in *Source 2* to make a chart like the one below in your exercise-book.
2. Describe the "ideal" candidate for the White House and a person with poor chances of being elected *(Source 3)*?
3. Based on information given in *Sources 1–3*, name some of the problems concerning equal rights which still lay ahead of the new nation in 1787.

- 42 men
- 42 whites
- 41 Protestants
- 35 born east of the Mississippi River
- 41 married
- 39 with British ancestors
- 28 academics (mostly lawyers)
- 27 from the North

SOURCE 3: The first 42 presidents of the USA

Person (location in picture)	Approximate time in history	Right to vote in national elections? Yes	No	Reason
well-dressed man (far right front)	1700s	X		probably land-owner
black slave (far left back)	before 1860		X	not a citizen
…				

The Industrial Revolution

1 Introduction: A time of change – changing views of a city

SOURCE 1: A view of Leeds in 1715

SOURCE 2: A view of Leeds in 1858

The changing views of a town:

1. Describe the views of Leeds in 1715 (Source 1) and 1858 (Source 2). What are the differences? The words on the right will help you.
2. Talk about the changes between 1715 and 1858. Think of energy, machines, money, people.
3. What do Sources 2 and 3 have in common, in contrast to Source 1? Look especially at the size of Leeds and at the buildings. What are your conclusions?

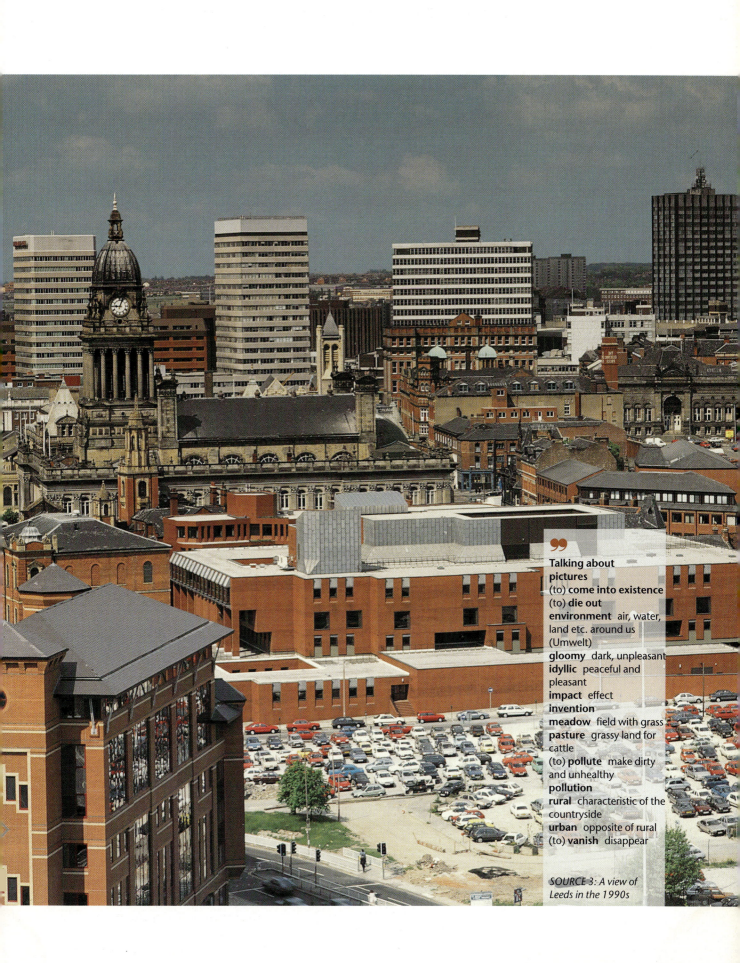

> **Talking about pictures**
> (to) **come into existence**
> (to) **die out**
> **environment** air, water, land etc. around us (Umwelt)
> **gloomy** dark, unpleasant
> **idyllic** peaceful and pleasant
> **impact** effect
> **invention**
> **meadow** field with grass
> **pasture** grassy land for cattle
> (to) **pollute** make dirty and unhealthy
> **pollution**
> **rural** characteristic of the countryside
> **urban** opposite of rural
> (to) **vanish** disappear

SOURCE 3: A view of Leeds in the 1990s

2 Developments in manufacturing and agriculture

2.1 Spinning, weaving and the beginnings of mass production

SOURCE 1: Spinners at work (c. 1814)

- spinning wheel
- cooking the yarn
- winding the yarn

▼▼▼
Source 1
- *(to) manufacture* produce
- *yarn* thread made of wool or cotton
- *(to) wind, wound, wound* [waind, waund, waund] make sth. long go round and round another thing

Source 2
- *loom* frame/machine for weaving cloth
- *shuttle* Weberschiffchen
- *spindle* Spindel

Source 3
- *lace* very fine cloth with a lot of holes in it

SOURCE 4: A cotton facto

The beginnings of industry:
1 Describe the work shown in *Sources 1 and 2*. Why do you think only women do the spinning?
2 Explain the differences in manufacturing between the first two pictures (*Sources 1 and 2*) and the following two pictures (*Sources 3 and 4*).
3 The people in the pictures cannot talk to us. If they could, what would they tell us?
4 Try to think of arguments in favour of the manufacturing system (→). What are the advantages of the factory system (→)? The words on the right will help you.

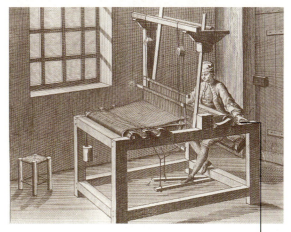
SOURCE 2: Weaving (c. 1762)

a hand-loom: The weaver holds the shuttle in his left hand.

SOURCE 3: The production of fine thread for lace-making

For and against the new system
opinion
• In my view/opinion …
• I'm of the opinion that …
• I doubt whether …
• I don't know …
• I'm not sure if …
• Many people would prefer to …
• Many would dislike the idea of …
atmosphere
• The picture gives the impression that …
• It suggests an atmosphere of …
• cosy comfortable, warm and friendly
• gloomy dark, depressing
• unpleasant not nice
• (to) estimate ['estɪmeɪt] guess sth.
production
• (to) feel under pressure
• (to) meet the demand
• (to) increase
• (to) go up

2.2 Progress in agriculture: Open and closed field systems, crop rotation

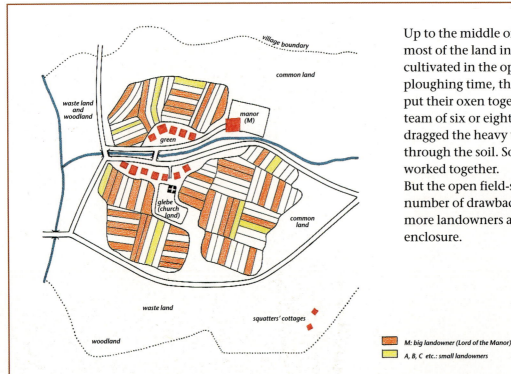

Up to the middle of the 18th century most of the land in England was cultivated in the open field-system. At ploughing time, the poorer farmers put their oxen together to make up a team of six or eight oxen which dragged the heavy wooden plough through the soil. So the villagers worked together.

But the open field-system had a number of drawbacks and more and more landowners adopted the idea of enclosure.

M: big landowner (Lord of the Manor)
A, B, C etc.: small landowners

SOURCE 5: A village before enclosure …

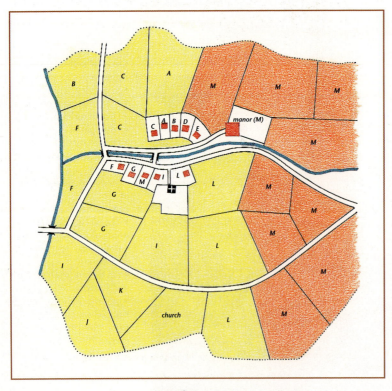

SOURCE 6: … and after enclosure
From the 13th century onwards more and more landowners adopted the idea of enclosure.

Providing the food:

1. Look at *Source 5*. Describe the arrangement of fields. The words on the right will help you.
2. Study *Sources 5–6* and point out the most striking changes.
3. Look again at *Source 5*. Imagine you're farmer A. Explain what your village is like. What problems do you have farming your land? What are the advantages of having strips of land in all the fields and of having the chance to use the common land?
4. Describe how the situation has changed for farmer A and the other villagers in *Source 6*. What are the benefits and the costs of the changes?

Enclosure was not the only change to take place in farming. In the Middle Ages the three field-system had been introduced. It replaced the simpler two-field system which worked by growing corn in one field and allowing the second field to lie fallow, i.e. not growing anything in order to restore the goodness to the soil again. The three field-system was an improvement, but still, every second or third year, one field was fallow land, as cereals like wheat and barley need rich soil.

The growing number of people living in bigger towns weren't able to produce their own food and had to rely on higher output and productivity from the farms. A new crop rotation system promised better results.

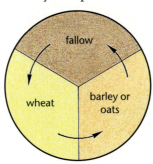

SOURCE 7: *The traditional rotation system*

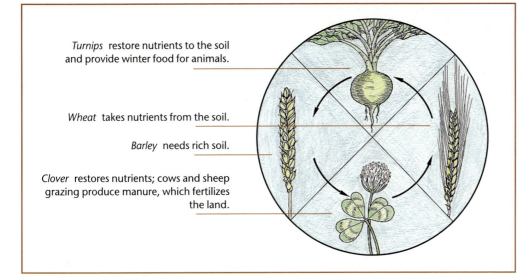

SOURCE 8: *The Norfolk Four-Course Rotation system*

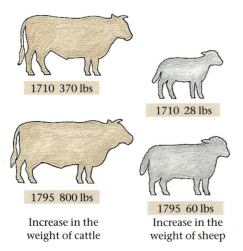

SOURCE 9: *Improvement in livestock breeding*

Exploiting the ground:
1 Describe the main differences between the traditional rotation system (Source 7) and the new Four-Course Rotation system (Source 8). Explain how the new system works over a period of several years.
2 What are the reasons for introducing the Four-Course Rotation system? Draw a series of diagrams illustrating the process over four years.
3 Relate the results of livestock breeding (Source 9) to the changes in cultivating the land, i.e. enclosures and the new Norfolk Four-Course Rotation system. Consider to what degree the Four-Course Rotation system supported the increase in productivity.

Some agricultural terms
land
• common land
• waste land
(to) divide up
• (to) ~ a field up into strips
• (to) rotate
size
• 10 yards wide
• 220 yards long
village
• villager
• cottage
animals
• cow
• sheep
• pig
• (to) keep cattle (on)
crops
• a crop (of) …
• cereals
• (to) grow barley/wheat/…

Source 5
• *enclosure* [ɪnˈkləʊʒə] piece of land that is surrounded by a fence or a wall
• *(to) drag* pull
• *weed* wild plant that grows where one does not want it to grow
• *squatter* poor peasant without land who pays no rent
• *breeding* producing young animals (Zucht)

Source 7
• *fallow land* land left uncultivated to restore its fertility
• *cereal* plant such as wheat, grown to produce grain
• *crop* plant such as grain, fruit or vegetables
• *barley* plant whose grain is grown for food (Gerste)
• *rotation* change

Source 8
• *turnip* round vegetable grown underground (Rübe)
• *clover* [ˈkləʊvə] small plant with pink or white flowers (Klee)
• *manure* [məˈnjʊə] waste matter from animals put on the ground to improve its quality
• *nutrient* [ˈnjuːtrɪənt] Nährstoff

Source 9
• *lbs* abbreviation for pound (weight)

2.3 Technological changes in agriculture

Sow four grains in a row,
One for the pigeon, one for the crow
one to rot, one to grow.

SOURCE 10: Farmer's rhyme

SOURCE 11: Ploughing in 1808

▼▼▼

Source 10
- *(to) sow, sowed, sown* [səʊ, səʊd, səʊn] put seed in or on the ground
- *pigeon* [ˈpɪdʒɪn] grey bird often seen in towns (Taube)
- *grain* seeds of a plant that we eat, e.g. wheat or rice
- *crow* [krəʊ] large black bird with a harsh cry (Krähe)

Source 13
- *triangular* having three straight sides and three angles
- *(to) rotate* turn around, change in a regular order
- *steadily* in an even, regular way
- *(to) trickle* flow in a thin stream

New methods of farming:

1 What does *Source 10* tell us about how well the old methods of sowing worked?
2 Seed drills such as the one shown in *Source 13* were used more and more often. Say what their advantages were.
3 Compare *Sources 11 and 12*. Describe the changes in ploughing and discuss the advantages of the steam plough.
4 Compare the ploughman's clothes *(Source 11)* with those of Jethro Tull *(Source 13)*. What does the difference in their clothing suggest?
5 Discuss how the quality of work has changed with the introduction of the steam plough.

SOURCE 12: Using a steam plough, c. 1900

6 Draw a diagram that shows some factors which led to what is called the *Agrarian Revolution*. Think in particular about changes in technology and land use.
7 Talk to a local farmer about technological changes in farming in the last fifty years.

SOURCE 13: *Jethro Tull and his seed drill.* – The triangular boxes were filled with seed, and as the wheels rotated, they operated a catch mechanism which allowed the seed to trickle steadily into the ground.

3 Changes in transport

3.1 Roads, rivers and canals

SOURCE 1: A carriage jolted to pieces

> On my journey to London, I travelled from Harborough to Northampton, and well was it that I was in a light berlin, and six good horses, or I might have been overlaid in that turnpike road. But for fear of life and limb, I walked several miles on foot, met twenty wagons tearing their goods to pieces and the drivers cursing …

SOURCE 2: Gentleman's Magazine (1747)

SOURCE 3: Transporting wool by pack horse

SOURCE 4: Stage wagon to carry goods

The Industrial Revolution 37

Anyone carrying heavy goods would use, as far as possible, the rivers and the sea. But using rivers had its problems, too. So in 1761 the Duke of Bridgewater had a canal built from Worsley in Lancashire, where he had coal mines, to Manchester. In the following years so many canals were built that people began to talk of a "canal mania".

SOURCE 5: Canal mania

◀ By land

By canal ▶

SOURCE 6: The cost of sending a ton of coal from Liverpool to Birmingham in 1790

▼▼▼

Source 1
• *(to) jolt* shake

Source 2
• *berlin* [bɜːˈlɪn] small coach with an open seat behind
• *overlaid* crushed to death
• *turnpike* road for which you have to pay

Source 6
• *navigable* [ˈnævɪɡəbl] deep enough for ships to sail on

3.2 Railways

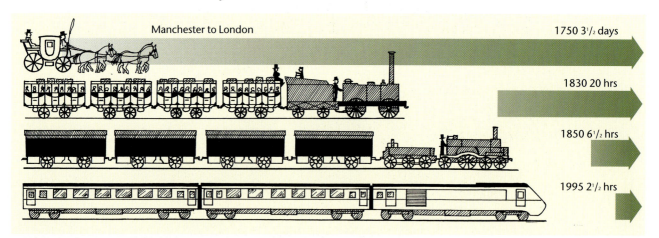

SOURCE 7: Speeding up

Manchester to London
- 1750 3½ days
- 1830 20 hrs
- 1850 6½ hrs
- 1995 2½ hrs

SOURCE 8: Coal wagon on a "plateway" (rails made of iron plates) in 1764

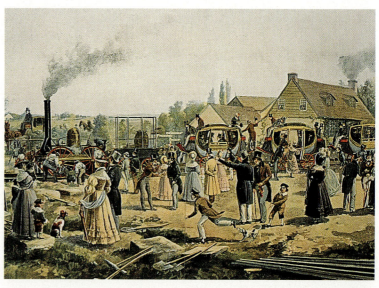

SOURCE 9: Opening of the Stockton to Darlington railway in 1825. The locomotive was built by George Stephenson.

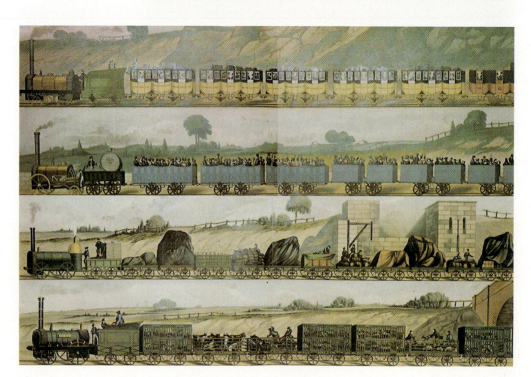

SOURCE 10: The Liverpool-Manchester railway was used for various purposes

SOURCE 11: A railway advertisement from the 1840s

SOURCE 12: "King Hudson's Levee" (Punch, 1845): George Hudson, known as the "Railway King" in the 1840s. He made a fortune by investing in railways.

Transport by road or by water:

1. Describe the situation of road transport in the second half of the 18th century (Sources 1–4). Why was this situation a great drawback in view of the changes in manufacturing, farming and population growth (see p. 48)?
2. Compare roads and canals.
   a. In the 18th century rivers were usually a better system of communication than roads. State how far this was true (Sources 5–6).
   b. "Building canals was a great improvement in transport." Describe the advantages of canals over rivers. The words on the right will help you.
   c. Canals had their shortcomings too. Try to name them.
3. "Good transport and communications are a vital aspect of modern life." Discuss this statement.

Transport by train:

4. Study Sources 7–10 and explain why railways were called *the* epoch-making transport innovation. Think especially of the following aspects: speed, weather, costs. Take Source 12 into account, too.
5. Source 11 suggests a new development in what the railway was being used for. Explain it.
6. Analyse the cartoon which underlines the importance of railways in an ironic way (Source 12). The clues will help you. Pay special attention to the position of the people. Then look up George Hudson in the biographies.
7. Discuss the role of railways, roads and canals, with today's ecological problems in mind.

Some terms related to transport

The role of transport
- (to) send bulky goods ['bʌlki]
- bulky goods things which are big and difficult to carry
- (to) carry heavy items
- (to) meet the growing demand
- (to) supply food for
- (to) provide the raw material
- (to) sell products over a wide area

advantages
- in large quantities
- cheap
- reliable [rɪ'laɪəbl] able to be trusted

transport by canal
- level of the water
- current ['kʌrənt] water that is moving

4 Using new materials and resources

4.1 Cotton

SOURCE 1: Cotton plant

SOURCE 2: Labels

Since the Middle Ages, England had been famous for its woollen cloth industry. In the 1750s however, there was a growing demand, both in Britain and Europe, for cotton textiles, and prizes were being offered in the early 1760s to encourage inventions which would increase the productivity of the spinner and the quality of the yarn.

SOURCE 3: An extract from
The First Industrial Revolution
(Ph. Deane)

"spinning jenny" 1763

SOURCE 4: Inventions in spinning

spinning "mule" 1779

modern spinning

▼▼▼
Source 1
• *blossom* ['blɒsəm] flower, especially of a fruit tree or flowering shrub (Blüte)
• *bud* [bʌd] flower or leaf not fully open (Knospe)
• *petal* ['petl] any of the delicate, coloured, leaf-like divisions of a flower (Blütenblatt)
• *stem* [stem] part of a plant, bush or tree coming up from the roots, from which the leaves or flowers grow (Stiel, Stamm)
• *leaf, leaves* [liːf, liːvz] flat, green parts of a plant that are joined to its stems or branches

Source 2
• *label* Wäschezeichen

Source 3
• *cloth* Stoff

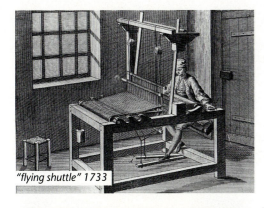
"flying shuttle" 1733

modern weaving

power loom 1784

SOURCE 5: Inventions in weaving

prices of cotton yarn		
1786/7	38s	per lb
1800	10s	per lb
1807	6s 9p	per lb

import of cotton	
1764	less than 4 mill lb
1833	more than 300 mill lb

price of a length of cotton cloth	
1770	£ 29
1812	13s
1860	5s

SOURCE 6

Cotton makes the wheels turn round:

1 Describe the cotton plant (→) and its fruit (*Source 1*). Then follow its way to cotton cloth. Copy the flowchart and fill in the boxes with the help of the information given in the glossary.

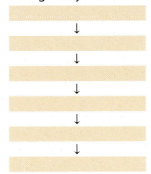

2 Read *Source 2*. Say what the advantages of cotton clothes are compared to other clothes.
3 *Source 3* talks about a growing demand for cotton textiles. What could be the reasons for the growing demand?
4 Describe the improvements brought about by new inventions in spinning and weaving (*Sources 4–5*). How were they connected and how did they influence each other? The words on the right will help you.
5 What do the data in *Source 6* tell you about the development of the cotton industry?
6 Use the Glossary and other information to find out something about the importance of cotton in British industry today.
7 Go to a local museum and find some (practical) information on weaving.

Some terms used in spinning
parts
• turning wheel Schwungrad
• spindle ['spɪndl] thin rod on which thread is twisted or wound (Spindel)
• yarn Garn
• twisted wound round and round
• (to) wind, wound, wound [waɪnd, waʊnd, waʊnd]
advantages
• at the same time ...
• simultaneously [ˌsɪml'teɪnɪəslɪ]
• better supply of ...
• ready for weaving

Some terms used in weaving
parts
• shuttle (Weber-)Schiffchen
• gears a set of wheels
how it works
• (to) pull a string
• (to) make hammers knock the shuttle back and forth
• (to) move the shuttle
advantages
• less force needed
• wider cloth
• steam power

4.2 Careers in cotton

1723	The Peels, a family of yeoman peasants in Lancashire, made a living from farm and textile production. Robert Peel (the elder) sold his goods in the countryside before moving into the town of Blackburn.
1750	Robert's son (Robert) born.
1760	Robert (the elder) mortgaged his land for about 3,000 pounds and founded a calico-printing firm with his brother-in-law and a man called Yates, who brought into it the accumulated savings of his family's innkeeping business. The family had experience: several members were in textiles.
c. 1765	The firm started to manufacture cloth itself as the demand for cotton to print on was high.
1772	The firm prospered and divided up: Peel remained in Blackburn, while his two partners moved to Bury. There they were joined in partnership by Robert Peel (the younger), with some help from his father at the beginning, but no support later on. Wealthy local men were anxious to invest in the growing industry and helped Peel (the younger) to raise additional capital.
c. 1785	The printing side of the firm alone made steady profits of 70,000 pounds a year for long periods. New devices such as steam engines were made use of in the firm. During the Napoleonic Wars, Robert Peel strongly supported state control of the working conditions of children in factories. There was fierce competition among cotton manufacturers, many of whom exploited their workers unscrupulously.
1790	Robert Peel was made a baronet (Sir Robert Peel) and became a member of Parliament. Though an affluent entrepreneur, he did not retire.
1830	Sir Robert Peel died. He left almost one and a half million pounds – a vast sum for those days. His son was about to become Prime Minister.

SOURCE 7: The career of the Peel family

SOURCE 8: The house of Sir R. Peel (the elder) in Blackburne, Lancashire

▼▼▼

Source 7
- *Yeoman peasant* ['jəʊmən 'peznt] farmer with land of his own
- *(to) mortgage* ['mɔːgɪdʒ] borrow money, esp. from a bank
- *calico* kind of cloth (Kattun)
- *affluent* wealthy
- *entrepreneur* [ˌɒntrəprə'nɜː] businessman

Source 11
- *(to) hire out* give the use of a person for payment
- *pauper* person living in a workhouse
- *apprentice* person who works for sb. who can teach him the skills of the trade
- *s* abbreviation for shilling
- *Justice of Peace (JP)* a judge in a small local court
- *debtor's prison* a prison for people who can't pay the money they owe to sb.

SOURCE 9: Old Drayton Hall built by the first Robert Peel

The road to success:
1 Describe how the Peels' success is reflected in their new residence (Sources 8–9). Talk about possible changes in their lifestyles.
2 Read Source 7. Discuss the following statement: The Peels, father and son, fulfilled all the requirements for a successful career in manufacturing as regards family background, education, experience, connections with important people.
   a Consider what qualities you need to be a successful entrepreneur? The words on the right will help you.
   b Which of these terms on the right could apply to the Peels (Source 7)?
3 What more information do we need to find out what kind of people the Peels were?
4 Collect some information about early industrialists in your region.

Cotton – a bumpy road:
1 Summarize all the information given on Blincoe on the title page (Source 10).
2 On the front page John Brown stresses the fact that the book was "the first memoir of the kind published". What was so unusual about the memoirs of a factory worker?
3 Look at Source 11 and explain how Blincoe tried to improve his working conditions in the factory and why he failed.
4 Compare the careers of the Peels with Blincoe's career. Take into account the information about their origins, their connections and their financial means.

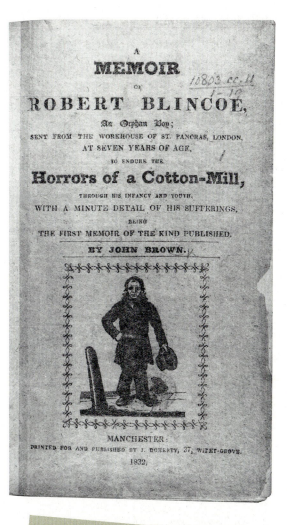

Some terms useful for describing people
doubtful ['daʊtfl] not certain
determined [dɪ'tɜːmɪnd] very certain that you want to do sth.
curious ['kjʊəriəs] wanting to know or learn
ruthless ['ruːθlɪs] having or showing no pity or compassion
caring giving care and support to sb./sth.
kind-hearted
cautious ['kɔːʃəs] careful
conservative against sudden change
open-minded
hard-working
generous
thrifty careful with money
ready to take risks
greedy wanting/taking more than you need
ambitious [æm'bɪʃəs] wanting to do well

SOURCE 10: The second edition of Blincoe's Memoirs

c. 1792	Robert Blincoe born and abandoned by his parents; grew up in St. Pancras Workhouse, London.
1799	His workhouse hired out 70–80 of its pauper children to Lowdham Cotton Mill, as apprentices.
1802	Parliament passed a bill for the protection of pauper children in cotton mills, but it was never applied in Lowdham Cotton Mill.
1803	Lowdham closed down; the "apprentices" were hired out to Litton Mill. Conditions there were even worse. An epidemic broke out; many of the children died from diarrhoea and high fever, only to be replaced by new arrivals. The doctor, a friend of the mill's owner, prescribed better food, but didn't inform the authorities. Blincoe refused to go on working and was badly beaten; his report to a Justice of Peace made things worse, because his employer was informed by the JP about Blincoe's complaint.
1812	He finished his apprenticeship at the age of 20 and worked in different cotton mills at 9–13 s a week.
1817	With his savings he set up a little trade in raw and scrap cotton in Manchester. After losing nearly all his money in the first year, he regained his capital the year after and made a profit of £ 5.
1819	He got married and set up a shop.
1822	Blincoe was interviewed by John Brown, a journalist from Bolton, who later published Blincoe's memoirs.
1824	With his profits Blincoe bought some old spinning machines and a factory building, but they were destroyed by a fire.
1827	His name appeared in the register of the debtor's prison in Lancaster.
1830	He was back in trade with scrap cotton and owned a small shop. None of his three children worked in a factory.
1843	He was last mentioned in the Manchester trade register.
1860	Blincoe died.

SOURCE 11: Life of a cotton mill worker (taken from Blincoe's memoirs)

4.3 Iron and coal

▼▼▼

Source 12
- *charcoal* ['tʃɑːkəʊl] fuel made by burning wood in a closed container with little air (Holzkohle)
- *slag* material left when metal is separated from rock (Schlacke)

Source 13
- *coke* fossil fuel (Koks)
- *furnace* ['fɜːnɪs] a smelting oven (Schmelzofen)
- *bellows* instrument producing a stream of air (Blasebalg)
- *blast* sudden movement of air (Luftstoß)

Source 17
- *pulley* ['pʊlɪ] Rolle
- *rope* [rəʊp] Seil, Tau
- *wagon* ['wægən] Wagen
- *basket* ['bɑːskɪt] Korb
- *shaft* [ʃɑːft] Schacht
- *working* Stollen

SOURCE 12: *How iron used to be made (1556)*

1708 Coal could be made into coke which burnt at a very high temperature. Coal was found in large amounts in many places in Britain. Charcoal became superfluous.

c. 1750 A new kind of furnace produced purer iron.

c. 1790 Steam engines were used for bellows instead of water wheels: they produced a very strong blast.

c. 1750 Canal system to transport coal and iron was established.

SOURCE 13: *Important changes*

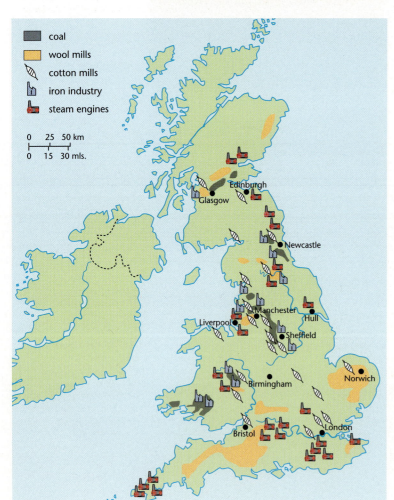

SOURCE 14: *Coal- and iron-producing areas in Britain*

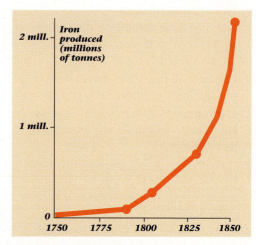

SOURCE 15: *Annual iron production*

Coal Production, 1700-1850	
Year	Amount of coal, in millions of tonnes
1700	2.9
1750	5.3
1775	8.9
1800	15.2
1815	22.6
1830	30.8
1850	65.7

SOURCE 16: *Annual coal production*

Iron production and coal mining:

1 *Source 12* shows you the traditional way of smelting iron. Consult the entry on iron in the glossary to describe the different activities in the illustration.
2 Study the changes and inventions listed in *Source 13* and point out how they improved the production of iron.
3 Examine the location and distribution of coal- and iron-producing areas in Britain *(Source 14)*.
   a What could this mean for the transportation and the production costs of British iron?
   b Say what the connection is between what you have discovered and the presence of cotton mills and steam engines.
4 Look at *Source 16*. Transfer the data from *Source 16* onto a line graph. (Look at the HISTORY SKILLS-box on p. 47). Compare it with the line graph in *Source 15*.
5 Describe some of the various operations in the coal-mine *(Source 17)*. The words on the right will help you.
6 Relate the operations shown in *Source 17* to the accident statistics *(Source 18)*. Point out the risks of a miner's job. Take into account the relevant *Sources* on pp. 51–53.
7 Evaluate the technological changes presented in *Source 19*. Think especially about productivity and safety in the coal-mines. Relate them to the growing use of iron and steam.

SOURCE 17: *An English coalmine at the beginning of the 19th century*

Cause of accident	Number of accidents	Number of deaths
Explosions	87	1243
Suffocation by gases	4	18
Flooding from old workings	4	83
Falling of earth	15	33
Chains or ropes breaking	19	45
Being run over by wagons	13	12
Boilers bursting	5	34
Total	147	1468

SOURCE 18: *Numbers of deaths in the Durham and Northumberland coalfields between 1799 and 1840*

Describing a coalmine
actions
- (to) lower
- (to) raise
- (to) push
- (to) pull
- (to) load put things on sth. that will carry them
- (to) drag pull with difficulty
- (to) cut the coal
- (to) crawl
- (to) dig
- (to) pump
- wagon containing coal

tool
- pickaxe ['pɪkæks] tool with curved piece of metal and long wooden handle, used for breaking up rocks or the ground

conditions
- narrow ['nærəʊ] not far from one side to the other
- confined [kən'faɪnd] limited in space
- strenuous ['strenjʊəs] needing great effort
- dark
- risky
- polluted air
- (to) be cut off from …

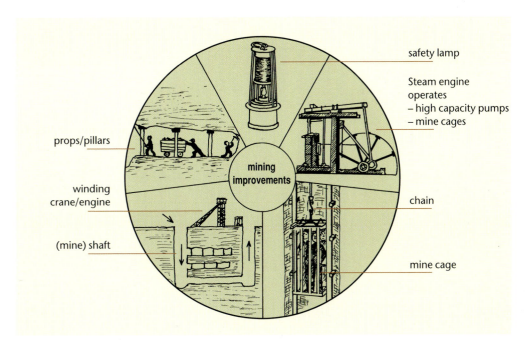

SOURCE 19: *Mining improvements*

4.4 Steam: a new source of energy

SOURCE 20: *A steam engine based on James Watt's invention*

Some technical terms
parts
- valve [vælv] mechanical device for controlling the flow of air, liquid or gas in one direction only
(to) open a ~
(to) close a ~
- lower cylinder ['sɪlɪndə]
- upper cylinder
- inlet opening to allow especially water or other liquid to enter
- outlet opening to allow especially water or other liquid out
- cogwheel a toothed wheel
- gears [gɪəz] a set of wheels that work together in a machine
- rod thin straight piece of wood or metal

motion
- up-and-down ~
- back-and-forth ~
- rotary ~ ['rəʊtərɪ] moving in a circular way
- The ~ is transmitted/passed on by … to …

processes
- A rod connects …
- Steam enters and exits …
- (to) push up and down
- (to) turn a wheel
- (to) condense [kən'dens] become liquid by cooling down
- (to) heat up
- (to) produce
- (to) lead to
- This causes the … to …
- First …, then …

The steam engine – a revolution in technology:

1. Describe from your own experience (think of the lid on a pot of boiling water!) what kind of motion steam produces. How is that motion altered in Watt's steam engine *(Sources 20–21)*?

2. The new engine with its turning wheel was soon used for many different purposes. Can you think of some? (The sections on cotton, agriculture, iron and coal, and on transport will give you some ideas.)

3. Understanding and describing the new technology of the steam engine:
   a Follow the different mechanical steps by which steam makes the wheel of the steam engine turn *(Source 21)*. Explain the term "sun and planet" gears.
   b Look at *Source 21*. It shows you how "double action" works. Describe the flow and action of the steam, starting with the opening of valves C and A. What advantages does this have compared with the "simple action" of earlier machines?

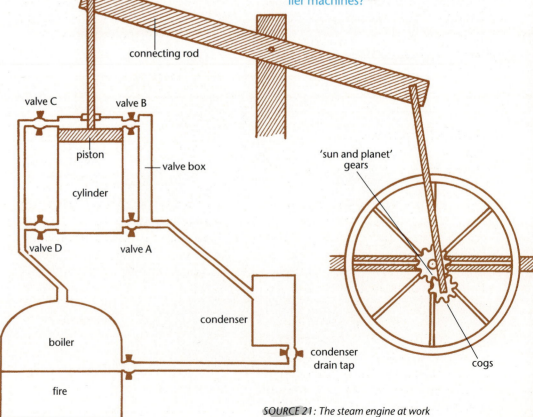

SOURCE 21: *The steam engine at work*

The steam engine is the mainspring of British industry, which urges it onwards and never allows it to lag or loiter.

There are many engines made by Boulton and Watt, forty years ago, which have been continually at work ever since with very few repairs. What a great number of horses would have been worn out doing the service of these machines! And what a vast quantity of grain they would have consumed. If British industry had not been aided by the steam engine, it would have been unable to advance because of the price of horses and the shortage of waterfalls.

Steam engines multiply industry. They create a vast demand for fuel; and while they provide power to drain the pits and raise the coals, they also give employment to miners, engineers, shipbuilders and sailors, and cause the construction of canals and railways. At the same time, they leave the rich farming land to produce food for people, not horses. Also, steam engines produce cheap goods for export, and enable us to buy in exchange both necessaries and comforts produced in foreign lands.

SOURCE 22: Andrew Ure (1835) on the importance of the steam engine

The mainspring of industry:
1. Copy the flow chart on the right into your exercise book and try to complete the boxes using key words from *Source 22*.
2. Make a list of the verbs in the text. You will find that most of the verbs personify the steam engine. Discuss the effects of personification.
3. If the text *(Source 22)* had been written today, what invention would we put in instead of "steam engine"?
   a Rewrite the text in groups, using the new term. Try to stick as closely to the original text as you can.
   b Read it out to the class and explain your changes. Does your new text share the optimism of *Source 22*? Give reasons.

History Skills

Analysing charts
Graphs, bar charts and pie charts are used to present data visually with the intention of making the information easy to understand.

A **graph** shows how (usually two) different values are related to each other.

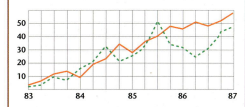

A **bar chart** is another way of showing changes in amounts, e.g. of population or profits, which is similar to a graph but uses rectangular shapes (= bars) instead of a line or curve.

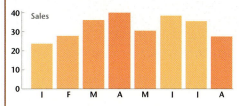

A **pie chart** is a diagram consisting of a circle (= pie) divided into sections that represent specific parts of the whole.

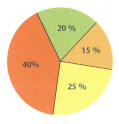

A **flow chart** consists of a drawing in which shapes and connecting lines are used to show the cause and effect-relationship of an event or a situation.

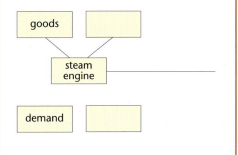

Source 21
• *valve* Ventil
• *connecting rod* Pleuelstange
• *piston* Kolben
• *drain* Abfluß
• *tap* Hahn
• *rod* Stange, Stab
• *gears* Getriebe; Gangschaltung

Source 22
• *mainspring* the chief force
• *(to) urge* [ɜːdʒ] encourage, make sb. do sth.
• *(to) allow* [əˈlaʊ] let sth. happen, make sth. possible
• *(to) lag* [læg] fall behind, go too slow
• *(to) loiter* [ˈlɔɪtə] wait around in an idle way
• *(to) wear out* [weə] become exhausted, thin or damaged through use
• *vast* enormous
• *(to) aid* [eɪd] help, support
• *(to) advance* [ədˈvɑːns] make progress, develop
• *(to) create* [kriːˈeɪt] make sth. new
• *(to) provide* [prəˈvaɪd] give sth. to sb. who needs it
• *(to) raise* [reɪz] move sth./sb. up
• *(to) produce* [prəˈdjuːs] make or grow sth.
• *(to) multiply* increase greatly
• *fuel* Brennstoff
• *(to) drain* remove water from
• *(to) enable* [ɪˈneɪbl] make it possible for sb. to do sth.
• *comforts* Luxusgüter

5 The situation of the working class

5.1 A growing population and expanding towns

SOURCE 1: Population growth in England, Wales and Scotland (in millions)

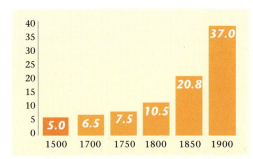

Year	Births	Deaths
1730	32.0	33.8
1790	35.2	25.8
1840	32.8	21.5

SOURCE 2: Births and deaths in England and Wales (per 1,000)

a Marriage and marriage age
- Percentage of unmarried people in the first half of the 18th century: decrease from 15% to about 7%.
- Average age for first marriages in England:

	Male	Female
1700–1749	28	27
1800–1849	26	24

b Medical knowledge

1798	Edward Jenner introduced small pox vaccine
1847	James Simpson, professor of midwifery, demonstrated anaesthesia with chloroform
1865	Joseph Lister practised antiseptic surgery

SOURCE 3: Marriage and changes in medicine

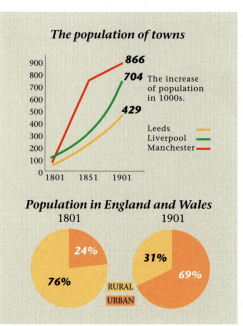

SOURCE 4: Towns and countryside

▼▼▼

Source 3
- *midwifery* knowledge of helping women give birth to children
- *anaesthesia* [ænisˈθiːziə] the use of pain-killing drugs in medicine
- *antiseptic* preventing infection
- *surgery* [ˈsɜːdʒəriː] the performing of medical operations

Source 6
- *refuse* [ˈrefjuːs] Müll

Source 7
- *damp* rather wet
- *drainage* [ˈdreɪnɪdʒ] system of pipes to carry water or waste from a place
- *corded frame* frame consisting of strings
- *(to) accumulate* [əˈkjuːmjʊleɪt] make or become greater
- *filth* [ˈfɪlθ] disgusting dirt
- *flax mill* mill where flax (a type of cotton) is used to produce linen
- *straw* [strɔː] dry stems of plants like wheat, barley etc. used as bedding and food for animals (Stroh)

Population growth and its consequences:

1 Describe the population development in *Source 1*. Distinguish between the period from 1500 to 1700 and from 1750 to 1900. Remember the HISTORY SKILLS box on p. 7.
2 Use the information given in *Source 2* to draw a graph. Draw a solid line for the birth rate and a dotted line for the death rate. Explain the differences between the two lines (cf. HISTORY SKILLS box).
3 *Sources 2–3* give you some of the reasons for the development shown in *Source 1*. Explain what the reasons are.
4 How does *Source 4* complete the information given in *Source 1*? Consider especially the increase of population in towns.

HISTORY SKILLS

Describing and explaining charts:
The **solid** line (——) shows the **increase/growth** of … from … to …

There is a **sharp/sudden** rise between …

The **increase/growth** of population of … **shown/indicated** by the **dotted/broken** line (…) and that of … indicated by the **broken** line (- - -) differs from …

In …, the **sector** that is **hatched** (parallel lines) shows the percentage of people that live/living …

5.2 Living conditions of the urban poor

SOURCE 5: Street in Glasgow (1900)

Number of workers' houses inspected: 6951; out of this number, houses ...

requiring repair	960
being damp	1435
wanting lavatories	2221
containing human refuse and other rubbish	352

SOURCE 6: From Dr Kay's Housing Survey of Manchester in 1832

I have been in one of those damp cellars without the slightest drainage, every drop of wet and every [piece] of dirt having to be carried up into the street; two corded frames for beds ... for five persons; [hardly] anything in the room to sit on but a stool, or a few bricks; the floor, in many places, absolutely wet; a pig in the corner also; and in a street where filth of all kind had accumulated for years. In another house (where the people were unable to pay the rent), I found a father and a mother and their two boys, both under the age of sixteen years, the parents sleeping on similar corded frames, and the two boys upon straw on the floor upstairs; never changing their clothes from week's end, working in the dusty department of a flax mill. ...
... The houses are [...] unprovided with toilets, and in consequence the streets which are narrow [and] unpaved [...], become the common resting place of mud, refuse and disgusting rubbish.

SOURCE 7: Report by Robert Baker, a Leeds surgeon and factory inspector, on local Irish cellar dwellings (1842)

SOURCE 8: Houses with separate cellar dwellings in Merthyr Tydfil, Wales

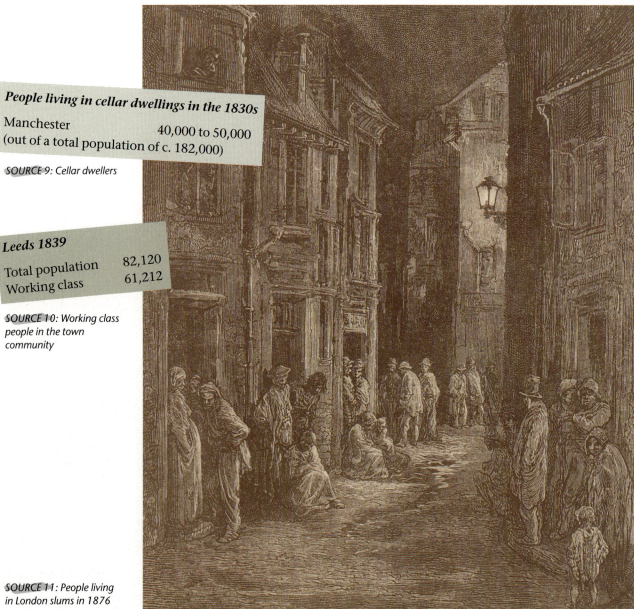

People living in cellar dwellings in the 1830s

Manchester 40,000 to 50,000
(out of a total population of c. 182,000)

SOURCE 9: Cellar dwellers

Leeds 1839

Total population 82,120
Working class 61,212

SOURCE 10: Working class people in the town community

SOURCE 11: People living in London slums in 1876 (etching by Gustave Doré)

Average age of death		
	Manchester	Rutland (rural area)
Professional families	38	52
Trade families (farmers, shopkeepers)	20	41
Working families	17	38

SOURCE 12: From a report on the sanitary conditions of the poor (1842)

How to keep clean and healthy:
1. Look at *Sources 5–11*. List what seems to be characteristic of the living conditions of the urban poor. Take into account the following aspects in particular: living space, sanitation (toilets etc.), supply of water, refuse, diseases.
2. Describe the differences in the average age of death as shown in *Source 12*. What could be the reasons for these differences?
3. Etching – photograph – report: images of urban misery
    a Write a short text for *Sources 5, 7 and 8* from the point of view of a teenager.
    b Which medium (text, photo or picture) is most suitable for presenting the misery of the working class population.

5.3 Working conditions in mines and factories

SOURCE 13: A miner's drawing of his work place

The old and small mills are dirty, low-roofed, badly ventilated; there are no conveniences for washing or dressing; machinery is not boxed in; some of the rooms are so low that it is scarcely possible to stand upright.

SOURCE 14: From a factory report of 1833

Year	Men Number	Wage (weekly)	Women Number	Wage (weekly)	Children (under 14) Number	Wage (weekly)	Hours (per week)
1831	139	19s 10d	385	5s 3d	250	3s 3d	72
1840	135	21s 8d	478	6s 0d	409	2s 6d	66

SOURCE 15: Figures from a Leeds spinning mill in the 1830s

Fines   s.d.
Any spinner found with his window open 10
Any spinner found dirty at his work 10
Any spinner found washing himself 10
Any spinner heard whistling 10
Any spinner being five minutes after last bell rings 10
Any spinner having a little waste on his spindles 10
Any spinner being sick and not able to find another spinner to give satisfaction must pay for steam for the day ... 60

SOURCE 17: A list of fines published in a strike pamphlet by spinners at Tyldey (1823). The average weekly wage was 15 shillings in 1841.

The forefinger of his left hand was caught, and almost before he could cry out, off was the first joint ... he clapped the mangled joint, streaming with blood, to the finger and ran off to the surgeon who very calmly put the parts together again and sent him back to the mill.

SOURCE 16: Robert Blincoe (see p. 43) had an accident in a mill at Lytton

The labour force:
1. Describe the working conditions (Sources 13–16) and comment on the accident reported in Source 16.
2. Describe the change in the figures between 1831 and 1840 (Source 15). What strikes you about the figures?
3. Comment on the fines listed in Source 17. If employers could impose such fines what does this suggest about the workers' position?

Source 14
• *convenience* [kən'viːniəns] lavatory or toilet
• *boxed in* enclosed

Source 17
• *fine* money you must pay because you have done sth. wrong
• *s.d.* old money (shilling and pence)
• *joint* part of the body where two bones meet (Gelenk)
• *(to) clap* place quickly
• *mangled* crushed, cut to pieces
• *surgeon* ['sɜːdʒən] doctor

52 The Industrial Revolution

I was married at 23, and went into a colliery when I was married. [...] I can neither read nor write. I am a drawer, and work from 6 in the morning to 6 at night. Stop about an hour at noon to eat my dinner. [...] I get no drink. I have two children, but they are too young to work. I worked at drawing when I was in the family way. I know a woman who has gone home. [...] She has been taken to her bed, been delivered of a child and gone to work again.
[...] I have a belt around my waist, and a chain passing between my legs and I go on my hands and feet. [...] It is very hard work for a woman. The pit is very wet where I work, and the water covers our clog-tops always. [...]
I am tired when I get home at night. I fall asleep sometimes before I get washed.

SOURCE 19: 37-year-old Betty Harris giving evidence to a Parliamentary Commission in 1842

SOURCE 18: A miner's drawing of women in a coalmine

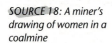

SOURCE 21: Photograph in a cotton mill in the 19th century

▼▼▼
Source 19
- *colliery* ['kɒlɪərɪ] coalmine
- *in the family way* pregnant
- *(to) deliver* (here) give birth
- *clogs* shoes made of wood

Source 20
- *bairn* baby
- *whistle* ['wɪsl] instrument used to produce a clear shrill sound
- *hissing* Zischen

Source 24
- *thread* [θred] long thin piece of cotton
- *(to) wipe down* make clean and dry with a cloth
- *machinery* a group of machines

Source 25
- *(to) strap* beat

Source 26
- *inconvenience* [ɪnkən'viːnɪəns] Unannehmlichkeit
- *(to) oblige* [ə'blaɪdʒ] (hier) entgegenkommen
- *(to) relieve* [rɪ'liːv] entlasten
- *(to) be supple* move easily
- *sallow* ['sæləʊ] unhealthy colour
- *rickets* ['rɪkɪts] disease that deforms the bones (Rachitis)
- *mischief* ['mɪstʃɪf] Unfug
- *habit* ['hæbɪt] sth. that sb. does very often (Gewohnheit)

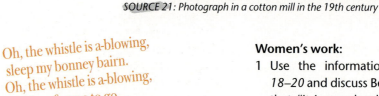

Oh, the whistle is a-blowing,
sleep my bonney bairn.
Oh, the whistle is a-blowing,
it's time for me to go,
Oh, the wheels they go a-turning
and the noise it makes you scream,
There's a-racing and a-going
and the hissing of the steam.

SOURCE 20: From a 19th-century song

Women's work:
1. Use the information given in *Sources 18–20* and discuss Betty Harris' statement that "it is very hard work for a woman" (Source 19).
2. Describe and discuss the emotional effect produced by the simple drawing (Source 18) and by the photograph (Source 21). The words on the right will help you.
3. What does the picture in *Source 21* suggest about the difference between a man's job and that of a woman?

SOURCE 22: The winding room of an early 19th-century cotton mill

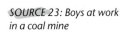

SOURCE 23: Boys at work in a coal mine

They can only be a certain size and under a certain age; they have to go under the threads to wipe down the machinery; if they are too large they break the threads and destroy the work. [...] As the machinery is at present constructed, only children 9 to 11 can do the work as it ought to be done.

SOURCE 24: Reasons for employing young children. A Parliamentary report from 1836.

Q Have any of your children been strapped?
A Yes, every one; including my eldest daughter. I was up in Lancashire a fortnight, and when I got back I saw her shoulders. She said, "The overlooker has strapped me; but", she said, "do not go to the overlooker, for if you do we shall lose our work."

SOURCE 25: A tailor from Leeds about his daughters' work in the mills

Q Could the mills be inspected without inconvenience?
A Certainly not. The attention of the children is drawn from their work by new faces, and inspectors would weaken the authority of the masters over the children.
Q Why do you take children so young?
A Partly to oblige the parents; to relieve the township; and because their figures are more supple and they can more easily be led into the habits of work.
Q Do children of six or seven work for ten and a half hours?
A Yes.
Q Have you ever found that children of six, seven, or eight years of age have sallow faces, rickets, or other signs of overwork?
A I do not live on the spot myself, but when I visit, I have always been satisfied with the state of health of the children.
Q Do you think that factory work is good for the morals of young people?
A Yes, so much so that it keeps them out of mischief, and while they are working they are less likely to get evil habits than if they are idle.

Q = Question/A = Answer

SOURCE 26: James Pattison, a factory employer from Congleton, on child labour

Talking about drawings and photographs
gloomy ['ɡluːmɪ] dark, badly lit
shock very unpleasant surprise, state of extreme weakness
sharp contrast ['kɒntrɑːst] clear difference between two things
lost not knowing where you are
surrounded by machines having machines all around you
helpless being unable to do things without help
steep [stiːp] rising or falling sharply
dangerous ['deɪndʒərəs] likely to cause danger
dusty ['dʌstɪ] covered in dust
in great detail very exactly
simplification
(un-)realistic

Children's work:
1 Study *Sources 24–26* and explain why child labour (→) seemed acceptable, necessary, and even desirable to many people during the Industrial Revolution:
2 Look at *Sources 22–26*.
  a Give your view on the kind of work done by children and their treatment *(Sources 22–23)*. Give reasons for your answer.
  b Comment on James Pattison's answer *(Source 26, l.3)*.
3 Find out about the problems of child labour today (UNESCO materials etc.).

54 ■ The Industrial Revolution

Talking about the cartoon
power and control
• strict/clear structure
• physical punishment
• aggressive [əˈgresɪv] ready to argue or fight with sb.
• cruel [ˈkruːəl] hurting other people or animals
• whip [wɪp] long piece of leather used to hit sb.
• (to) whip
• (to) bully [ˈbʊlɪ] hurt or frighten a weaker person
• factory owner [ˈfæktərɪ ˈəʊnə]
• supervisor [ˈsuːpəvaɪzə] a person (in a factory) who watches and checks that people are working properly
weakness
• weak
• fear
• afraid (of)
• scared
• slave [sleɪv]
• (to) look on watch an event or incident as a spectator
• (to) ignore
• monotonous [məˈnɒtənəs] very boring and uninteresting
• indifference
• (no) solidarity
• exhausted

Source 27
• *expenditure* amount of money sb. spends
• *lb* short for pound (0.45 kilograms)
• *loaf (pl. loaves)* [ləʊf, ləʊvz] (Laib) Brot
• *porter* [ˈpɔːtə] Portwein
• *cwt* a hundredweight (50.8 kilograms)
• *oz* ounce (28.3 grams)
• *sundries* various items

Source 29
• *restricted* [rɪˈstrɪktɪd] limited (beschränkt)

Source 30
• *shearing-frame* a machine for cutting off the fluff from newly-woven material

Source 32
• *bearer* owner, holder

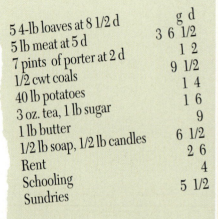

		g	d
5 4-lb loaves at 8 1/2 d		3 6	1/2
5 lb meat at 5 d		1	2
7 pints of porter at 2 d			9 1/2
1/2 cwt coals		1	4
40 lb potatoes		1	6
3 oz. tea, 1 lb sugar			9
1 lb butter		6	1/2
1/2 lb soap, 1/2 lb candles		2	6
Rent			4
Schooling		5	1/2
Sundries			

SOURCE 27: Family expenditure

SOURCE 28: John Cobden: The White Slaves, 1860

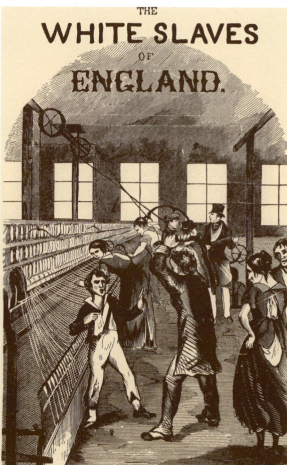

Year	Measure	What it Did
1842	Mines Act	Women, girls and boys under the age of ten not to work in mines. Inspectors to report on mines.
1844	Factory Act	Children from 8-13 restricted to working half the number of hours – 6 1/2 hours – before or after noon.
1847	Factory Act	People under 18 and all women only to work ten hours in one day.
1867	Factory Act	Brought most industries under the control of the Factory Acts.

SOURCE 29: Acts of Parliament

Toil and sweat and little in return:

1 A London worker in 1841 had regular earnings of 15 shillings a week to support himself and his family (wife and three children). What do the figures in *Source 27* tell us about the family's situation? Note what isn't included in the list and keep in mind that continuous employment wasn't guaranteed at all.

2 Study *Source 28* and look up the word "slave" in a dictionary and an encyclopedia. Talk about the picture from different points of view (owner, supervisor, worker) and discuss whether the expression "White Slaves" really describes the conditions of the workers.

3 Study the Acts of Parliament (*Source 29*) and point out the improvements. Compare the improvements with the situation of workers today.

5.4 The workers' struggle for change: Self-help or government reforms

The new machines made workers fear for their jobs and wages. Employers who used machines received letters like this signed with a made-up name: Ned Ludd, for protection.

> Sir,
> Information has just been given that you are a holder of those detestable shearing-frames and I was asked by my men to write to you, to give you fair warning to pull them down. If they are not taken down by the end of the week I shall send at least 300 men to destroy them.
>
> Signed   Ned Ludd

SOURCE 30: A Luddite letter

> They only broke the frames of such as have reduced men's wages. In one house last night they broke four frames out of six. The other two, which belonged to masters who had not lowered wages, they did not touch.

SOURCE 31: Report from the Leeds Mercury newspaper (1812)

SOURCE 32: Membership card of the Trade Union of Female Power Loom Weavers

SOURCE 33: The Cooperative Movement

Struggle for change:

1. In the preceding chapters you have examined a series of dramatic and rapid changes, some of which transformed the workers' lives in a radical way and often caused great distress. What attempts to get rid of these "dark sides" of industrialization can you remember?
2. *Sources 30–31* describe another way of reacting to the radical changes: Describe and evaluate the Luddites' actions.
3. Trade unions – first steps: Look at *Source 32*.
   a Comment on the motto of the society.
   b Name some of the functions of a membership card.
   c How does this union present itself?
4. Explain how the COOP movement (→) tried to help the workers (*Source 33*). Compare their ways of helping people with those of a trade union like the Female Weavers' Society (*Source 32*) and those of the Luddites (*Sources 30–31*). The words on the right will help you.

Protest and opposition
riot
• (to) riot
violence
• violent/non-violent
a threat
• (to) threaten
cooperation
mutual help
negotiation
• (to) negotiate
action
• legal ~
• illegal ~
demands
• (to) demand
• (to) present demands
strike
• (to) go on ~
party
• (to) found a ~
• (to) join a ~

After the Parliamentary Reform of 1832, men living in towns and holding property were allowed to vote. Working class people's interests were not yet represented in Parliament. So a group of tradesmen and small shopkeepers drew up a charter of political demands in 1838. It was presented in Parliament several times, and finally rejected in 1848.

▼▼▼

Source 34
- *(to) hold property* own a house, land etc.
- *charter* a written statement of principles, rights etc.
- *secret ballot* the right to vote without anybody watching
- *property qualifications* a certain amount of income or property
- *constituency* Wahlkreis
- *(to) defy* do sth. against sb.'s will
- *(to) betray* be unfaithful

Source 35
- *muskets* guns
- *(to) endure* [ɪnˈdʒʊə] suffer (ertragen)
- *(to) average* [ˈævərɪdʒ] durchschnittlich betragen

Source 37
- *share* Aktie

Source 38
- *householder* owner of a house or flat
- *lodger* person who rents a house or flat
- *franchise* the right to vote
- *rural workers* farm hands

Source 39
- *home rule* self-government/independence (here: for Ireland)
- *monopoly* control over production by a single person or group
- *landlordism* rule by sb. who owns land or houses and takes rent for them
- *temperance* Anti-Alkohol-

Source 40
- *emulation* Nacheifern
- *commonwealth* independent state, community
- *wealth* riches
- *toiler* hard worker

The Six Points OF THE PEOPLE'S CHARTER.

1. A VOTE for every man twenty-one years of age, unless he is mad or a criminal.

2. A SECRET BALLOT, to allow every man to vote in secret without fear.

3. NO PROPERTY QUALIFICATION to become a Member of Parliament – any man, rich or poor, can represent a constituency.

4. PAYMENT OF MEMBERS OF PARLIAMENT, so that any person can afford to leave his work to serve his country.

5. EQUAL CONSTITUENCIES, so that each Member of Parliament represents the same number of people.

6. ANNUAL ELECTIONS to Parliament, to stop corruption in elections and to make sure that Members of Parliament do not defy or betray those who vote for them.

SOURCE 34: Chartism

"A great many people were arming themselves with guns or picks. I bought a gun, although I knew it was a serious thing for a Chartist to have a gun in his possession. It might be said that we were fools, but young people now have no idea what we had to endure. From 1842 to 1848 I did not average 9 shillings (45p) a week."

SOURCE 35: Benjamin Wilson, an old Chartist, writing in 1887

"Muskets are not that are wanted, but education and schooling of the working people."

SOURCE 36: William Lovett (1800–1877), secretary of the London Working Men's Association

Workers for Parliament?

Year	Reform	Percentage of population over 21 allowed to vote
1832	new industrial towns elect MPs	7.1 %
1867	householders and lodgers in towns allowed to vote	16.4 %
1884	franchise for rural workers	28.0 %
1918	franchise for all men over 21 and women over 30	74.0 %

SOURCE 38: Parliamentary reforms

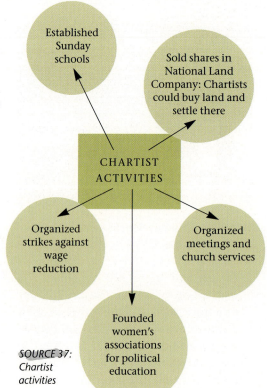

SOURCE 37: Chartist activities

A voice in Parliament:

1. Say in your own words what the six points of the Charter (Source 34) were, and what results they were expected to give.

2. What are the new elements in the aims of the Charter, compared to the aims of the Trade Unions and Cooperatives?

3. Some Chartists wanted to try different means (Sources 35 and 36). What were they? Compare them.

4. The Chartists did not succeed in their political aims, and all attempts at military uprisings were put down by the government. But still one might say that they were successful: Source 37 helps you to explain why.

5. Which of its points were accepted later in modern democracies (think of parliament, the Bundestag, and the electoral system).

The Industrial Revolution

SOURCE 40: Great expectations

SOURCE 39: Election poster for Keir Hardie, a working-class candidate (1895)

> **Analysing political slogans**
> **symbols**
> • allegory ['ælɪgərɪ] story, painting or description in which the characters and events are meant as symbols (of purity, truth, patience, etc.)
> • allegorical [ælɪ'gɒrɪkl]
> • fertility [fə'tɪlətɪ]
> • garland ['gɑːlənd] circle of flowers or leaves worn around the neck or head
> **clothing**
> • neo-classicist ~
> • antique ~
> • flowing ~
> • cap of liberty cap worn during the French Revolution by revolutionaries (Jakobinermütze)
> **working conditions**
> • (to) improve ~
> • child labour
> • working hours
> **political slogans/programmes**
> • socialist movement
> • solidarity between the people
> • internationalism
> • nationalism
> • protectionism
> • protectionist
> • profit
> • production
> • education for all
> • utopian world of happiness

Workers for Parliament:

1 Though the British government did not give in to the Chartist demands, it did accept the need for reforms. *Source 38* lists some of them. Say what they were and what effect they had on the representation of working-class interests in Parliament.

2 At the end of the 19th century, the first working-class parties appeared. Examine their beginnings.
   a Read the slogans K. Hardie uses (*Source 39*). Can you spot some new demands?
   b In 1906, the Labour Party was formed by K. Hardie's party, by the Trades Union Congress, and some other groups. Find out what political parties there are in Great Britain today.

3 *Source 40* shows you the hopes workers had for the new party.
   a Go through the list of slogans and sort out those which directly refer to aspects of previous chapters; give concrete examples (e.g. child labour).
   b Choose one or two slogans which express the vision for a happier future at the time. The words on the right will help you.
   c Discuss some of the slogans which would still appeal to people. Write some slogans which express workers' concerns today.

5.5 Another way out: Emigration

Free emigration to South Australia via Southampton

We are authorized by Her Majesty's Colonial Land and Emigration Commissioners to grant a free passage by first-class ship to the healthy and prosperous colony of South Australia, to agricultural labourers, sheperds, male and female servants, miners of good character. The demand for labour in the colony is urgent, with good pay ensuring the comfort of every well-conducted man and his family.

SOURCE 41: Advertisement in the Northhampton Herald, 1839

Now to all who intend to migrate
Come listen to this doleful fate
Which did befall me of late
When I went to the wilds of Australia.
I sailed across the stormy main
And often wished myself back again;
I really think I was quite insane
When I went to the bush of Australia.

And when I came to look at the land,
Which I got by His Excellency's command,
I found it nothing but burning sand
Like all the rest of Australia.
But I bought a flock of sheep at last,
And thought that all my troubles were past,
You may well believe that I stood aghast
When they died of the rot in Australia.

SOURCE 42: Anonymous 19th-century ballad

	1861–1870	1881–1890	Total 1851–1920
USA	442,000	1,008,000	4.651,000
Canada	90,000	257,000	2,856,000
Australia	184,000	317,000	2,102,000
Others	37,000	162,000	1,606,000
Total	753,000	1,124,000	11,215,000

SOURCE 43: Numbers and destination of people emigrating from Great Britain

---

A new start – promises, hopes and despair (Sources 41–45):

1 Emigration was an important factor in the history of the Industrial Revolution. Study the figures in *Source 43* and *Source 1* (p. 48) and discuss this statement in the light of the information given in these *Sources*. Before you start, familiarize yourself with the figures by comparing them to the current population of your home town, immigration figures for Germany, the USA and Australia today.

2 Statistics do not take account of the individual. Work in groups and look at the following suggestions which will help you understand the drama of leaving home. The words on the right will help you.
 a Look at *Sources 41, 42, 44, 45*. What do they tell you?
 b Invent a family who are preparing to take the dramatic step of emigrating (think of names, occupations, age, home town, destination etc.). Go through this chapter and collect relevant data (on housing, working conditions etc.).
 c Act out a discussion in the "family" based on *Sources 41–43* in which you weigh up the government's promises against the warnings in the ballad. Your "family" will have to come to a decision.
 d If your "family" or some of its members have decided to take the risk, turn to *Source 44* and identify "your characters". Write dramatic farewell scenes. Perhaps you could begin by making speech bubbles for the picture. Describe their arrival in the New World (*Source 45*), too.

3 Is emigration a solution? Give reasons for your answer.

SOURCE 44: An emigrant ship

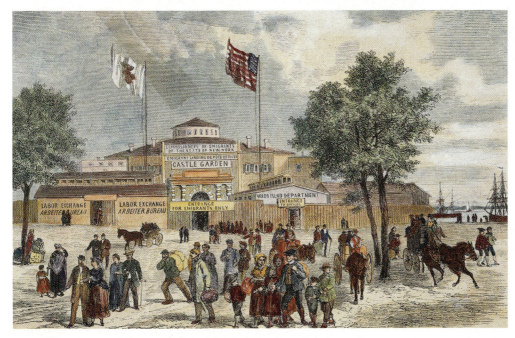

SOURCE 45: Arriving in the New World in 1870

hope, fear and despair
- hopeless
- There is no way out/no choice …
- We can't go on like this …
- We can/can't trust the government/…
- We have to/can't risk …
- I can't leave my …
- Think of the nice climate/wages/the great demand for workers/…

propaganda, promises and warnings
- They promise …
- We don't know much about Australia …
- It looks so simple/too good to be true …
- The ballad also tells a very simple story …
- Of course, there are going to be problems …
- We'll never have to worry about …
- You have to accept that there are going to be problems …
- It won't be easy
- We're starving here …

▼▼▼

Source 41
- *(to) authorize* ['ɔːθəraɪz] give official permission for sth. to happen
- *Commissioner* [kə'mɪʃənə] important official in an organization
- *(to) grant* [grɑːnt] give sth. formally or legally
- *prosperous* ['prɒspərəs] successful and wealthy
- *urgent* ['ɜːdʒənt] so important it has to be done immediately
- *(to) ensure* [ɪn'ʃɔː] make sure, guarantee
- *well-conducted* [ˌwel kən'dʌktɪd] well-behaved

Source 42
- *(to) migrate* [maɪ'greɪt] move from one place to go to live or work in another
- *doleful* ['dəʊfl] sad, miserable
- *main (poetic)* open sea
- *insane* [ɪn'seɪn] mad
- *flock* group of birds, sheep or goat
- *aghast* [ə'gɑːst] filled with horror or amazement
- *rot* liver disease of sheep

6 The change goes on: Progress or curse?

The future – for better or for worse?
1. Describe the festive atmosphere and splendour of the Exhibition building (Source 1). The words on the right will help you.
2. The World Exhibition in London (Sources 1–3) was a celebration of industrial progress. Form two groups and think of:
   a. products that could be presented,
   b. the dark side of industrial progress.

SOURCE 1: *The World Exhibition in London was opened by Queen Victoria and Prince Albert in 1851. It was meant to be "a showcase for modern industry", covering 8 hectares of ground and offering 13 kilometres of table space for the displays.*

"[…] the exhibition of 1851 is to give a true test and a living picture of the point of development at which the whole of mankind has arrived in this great task, and a new starting point from which all nations will be able to direct their further exertions […]"

SOURCE 2: *Prince Albert on the Exhibition*

"WHAT WILL HE GROW TO?"

SOURCE 3: *Sources of energy. King Steam and King Coal are watching Baby Electricity: "What will become of him and us? Will he be the last baby in the family?"*

▼▼▼

Source 1
- *display* attractive arrangement of different things, intended to attract people's attention

Source 2
- *exertion* [ɪɡˈzɜːʃn] effort

The Industrial Revolution 61

SOURCE 4: *Children working in a Columbian mine in the 1990s*

3 *Source 6* is taken from a science fiction story. The hero, Linter, seems to have fallen in love with our planet and wants to leave his spaceship to live on earth. He tells his friend Sma about his decision.

   a Before reading the text make a list of things that could make Earth an attractive place for an alien from a far superior culture and civilisation. Compare your list with a partner.

   b Before reading look at *Sources 4–5* and list some of the problems Western industrial culture is facing today. Compare your list with a partner.

   c Read the text in two groups – one group identifying with Linter's position (the fascination of change), the other using Sma's arguments against Linter's decision (the horrors of change). Role-play the situation between Linter and Sma.

SOURCE 5: *A modern car factory – robot arms at work*

Describing the Crystal Palace
The building
• grand [grænd] very big, important, magnificent
• magnificent [mæg'nɪfɪsnt] splendid, remarkable
• impressive
• height [haɪt]
• space
• statue
• steel
• glass
• light
• (to) decorate ['dekəreɪt]
• decoration
• chandelier [ˌʃændə'lɪə] magnificent light fitting which hangs from a ceiling
• crystal ['krɪstl]
• (to) glitter sparkle, shine brightly with a lot of light
• high roof
• gallery ['gæləri]
The people
• high society
• fine clothes
• smartly dressed
• occasion [ə'keɪʒn] special event or celebration; special ~, festive ~
• glamour ['glæmə]

Source 6
• *fluff* [flʌf] soft light stuff that comes off wool etc.
• *regardless* paying no attention to sb./sth.
• *(to) shrug* [ʃrʌg] move your shoulders to show that you do not know or care about sth.
• *challenge* ['tʃælɪndʒ] new or difficult thing that makes you try hard
• *unfazed* not surprised
• *snort* [snɔːt] Schnauben
• *the Culture* computer which is the president of the extraterrestrials
• *drained* emptied
• *eventually* schließlich
• *(to) alter* become different, change
• *available* [ə'veɪləbl] that can be used or obtained
• *(to) desert* [dɪ'zɜːt] go away from a place without intending ever to return

H e drew on the cigarette , studying me through the smoke. He crossed his legs and brushed some imaginary fluff off the trouser cuffs and stared at his shoes. "I've told the ship
5 when it leaves , I'm staying here on Earth. Regardless of what else might happen."
He shrugged . "Whether we contact or not." He looked at me, challenging.
"Any … particular reason?" I tried to sound un-
10 fazed. I still thought it must be a woman. "Yes. I like the place." He made a noise between a snort and a laugh. "I feel alive for a change. I want to stay. I'm going to live here."
"You want to die here?"
15 He smiled, looked away from me, then back. "Yes. Quite positively." This shut me up for a moment.
[…]
"… it is we who need them, not the other way
20 round." Linter turned and stared at me, but I wasn't going to start arguing on a second front now. "But," he said after a pause, "the Culture can do without me." He inspected his drained glass. "It's going to have to."
25 I was silent for a while, watching the television flip through channels. "What about you though?" I asked eventually. "Can you do without it?"
"Easily," Linter laughed. "Listen, d'you think I haven't –" 30
"No; you listen. How long do you think this place is going to stay the way it is now? Ten years? Twenty? Can't you see how much this place has to alter … in just the next century? We're so used to things staying much the same, 35 to society and technology – at least immediately available technology – hardly changing over our lifetimes that … I don't know any of us could cope for long down here. I think it'll affect you a lot more than the locals. They're used to 40 change, used to it all happening fast. All right, you like the way it is now, but what happens later? What if 2077 is as different from now as this is from 1877? This might be the end of a Golden Age, world war or not. What chance do 45 *you* think the West has of keeping the status quo with the Third World? I'm telling you; end of the century and you'll feel lonely and afraid and wonder why they've deserted you and you'll be the worst nostalgic they've got because you'll 50 remember it better than they ever will and you won't remember anything else from before now."

SOURCE 6: *An excerpt from the science fiction story* The State of the Art *by Iain M. Banks*

Imperialism

1   Introduction: Europe in Africa

> **Describing maps making assumptions**
> - It appears that …
> - It's obvious that …
> - It seems as if …
> - According to …
>
> **conflicts**
> - conflict fight or argument
> - rivalry ['raɪvlrɪ] competition,
> - political/religious/military ~
> - (to) quarrel about sth. ['kwɒrəl] argue about sth.
>
> **violence**
> - outbreak of ~
> - (to) break out start suddenly
> - (to) attack
> - (to) fight
> - fighting
> - (to) invade [ɪnˈveɪd] go into another country to attack it
> - invasion [ɪnˈveɪʒn]
> - (to) be armed have a weapon
> - guerilla [gəˈrɪlə] person who fights secretly against the government or an army
> - (to) take over gain control of sth.
>
> **nation**
> - nationality [ˌnæʃəˈnælətɪ]
> - tribe [traɪb] small group of people who have the same language and customs
> - border

SOURCE 1: A continent of conflicts

▼▼▼
Source 1
- *resentment* anger/bitterness about sth.
- *ethnic* having to do with a race of people
- *strife* fighting, quarrelling
- *tension* strain in a political or social relationship
- *coup d'état* overthrowing a government

Working with a contemporary source:
1. Look at the map (Source 1) and say what Africa's problems are. The words on the left will help you.
2. What could be the reasons for these problems? Discuss them from an African and European point of view.

Cape Coast – Ghana
Kruegerdorp – South Africa
Porto Alexandre – Angola
Nsukka – Nigeria
Lusambo – Zaire

SOURCE 3: African place names

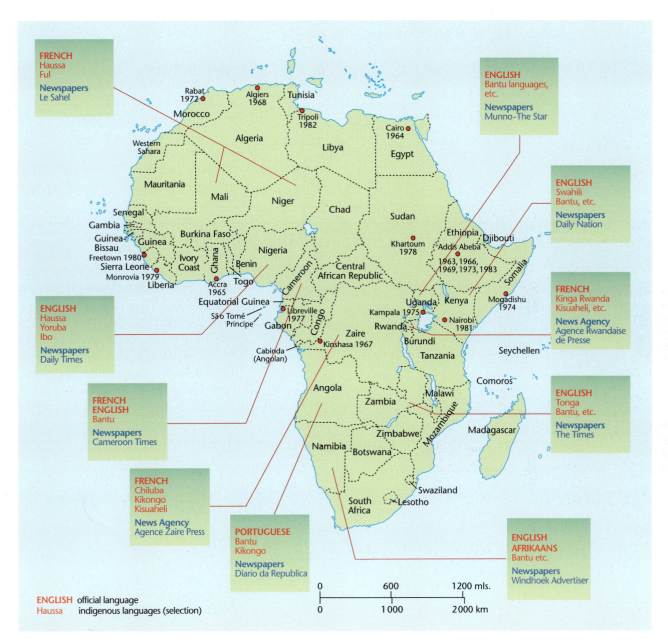

SOURCE 2: Languages in Africa today

Inhambane – Mozambique
Brazzaville – Congo
Marienthal – Namibia
Nova Lisboa – Angola

European languages in Africa:

1. Look at *Source 2*. What European languages are spoken in Africa? What could the reasons for the use of these languages be?
2. Study *Source 3*. What strikes you about this list of place names?
3. Now form smaller groups. Write down some questions related to Africa's situation as shown in *Sources 1–3*.

▼▼▼

Source 2
• **official languages** formal, recognized language of a country
• **indigenous languages** [ɪnˈdɪdʒɪnəs] native languages originating in a particular country, region etc.

• **related to** connected with

2 European expansion in Africa

2.1 Working with maps: Changes

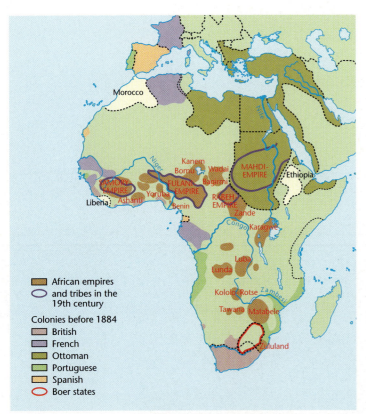

SOURCE 1: Africa around 1880
At the beginning of the 19th century Africa was a "white spot" on the globe for the Europeans; it was also called the "dark continent".

SOURCE 2: European colonies and anticolonial rebellions in Africa before 1914

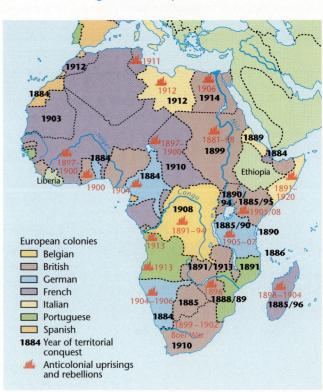

Going to Africa:
1. Look at *Source 1* and describe the political situation around 1880.
2. Describe where the Europeans settled and suggest why *(Source 1)*.
3. Explain the two expressions: "white spot" and "dark continent". Try to explain the terms from the point of view of a native African.
4. Study *Source 2* and use the map key to explain the changes around 1880.
5. Study *Source 3*.
   a Use the data in *Source 3* to draw a bar chart. The words on the right will help you.
   b Use the bar chart you have drawn to describe the development of each colonial power and look at the relationship between them. Think of possible consequences for the powers.
6. **Choose** a contemporary state from *Source 4*, collect information about the political and economic situation of this state and give a short report.

▼▼▼

Source 1
• *(to) suggest* put forward an idea

Source 4
• *acquisition* the act of gaining something
• *possession* sth. which is yours
• *(to) multiply* 3 multiplied by 2 is 6
• *(to) take the lead* be the first

Imperialism

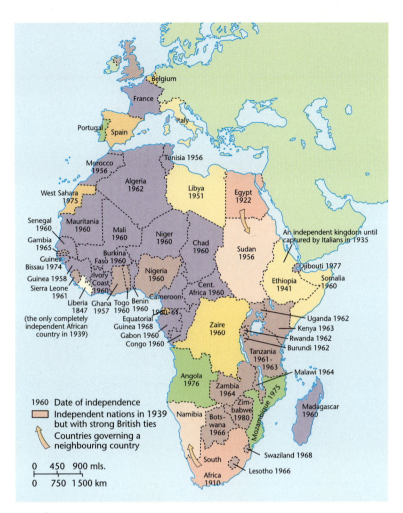

	1881	
Britain		670,953
Germany		0
3rd French Republic		320,972
	1895	
Britain		5,965,519
Germany		2,385,100
3rd French Republic		2,381,476
	1912	
Britain		6,209,602
Germany		2,657,300
3rd French Republic		6,480,200

SOURCE 3: Acquisition of colonial territory in Africa (in km²)

SOURCE 4: Independent Africa

History Skills

Historical maps
Historical maps show a situation at a certain period of time.

Describing a situation
The map shows ... (Use the map title and key.)

I / we	learn that the	land was / continent	inhabited by ... / populated

I / we	can see that ... was divided up between ...

Describing change and development

At first	the Europeans	settled / founded colonies	in ... / along ...
In the ... century			
Later they	conquered ... / took possession of ...		

> Describing a bar chart
chart
- box
- column
- dates
- possession
- (to) show the size of
- (to) strike sb.
- (to) multiply sth. by

increase and decrease
- (to) increase from ... to ...
- (to) overtake
- (to) take the lead
- (to) rise to
- (to) fall behind
- (to) catch up with

2.2 Reasons for imperialist expansion

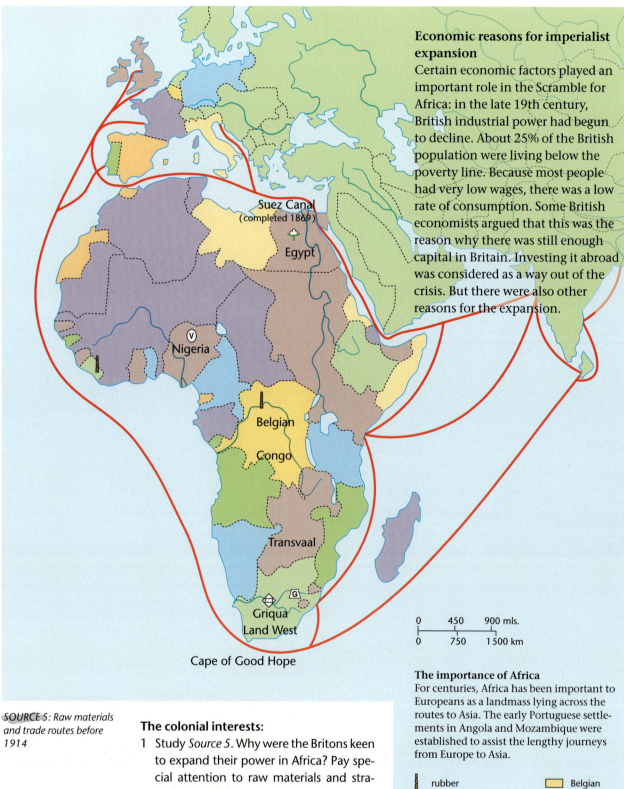

Economic reasons for imperialist expansion

Certain economic factors played an important role in the Scramble for Africa: in the late 19th century, British industrial power had begun to decline. About 25% of the British population were living below the poverty line. Because most people had very low wages, there was a low rate of consumption. Some British economists argued that this was the reason why there was still enough capital in Britain. Investing it abroad was considered as a way out of the crisis. But there were also other reasons for the expansion.

SOURCE 5: Raw materials and trade routes before 1914

The importance of Africa
For centuries, Africa has been important to Europeans as a landmass lying across the routes to Asia. The early Portuguese settlements in Angola and Mozambique were established to assist the lengthy journeys from Europe to Asia.

- rubber
- cotton
- vegetable oil
- gold – discovered in 1884
- diamonds – discovered in 1868

- Belgian
- British
- German
- French
- Italian
- Portuguese
- Spanish

The colonial interests:
1 Study *Source 5*. Why were the Britons keen to expand their power in Africa? Pay special attention to raw materials and strategic interests.
2 What could the cause and effect relationship (see p. 13) be between the economic situation inside Britain and British expansion in Africa and India? Take into account what you have learnt in the previous chapters.

Rhodes' vision of British rule in Africa:
1 Describe the cartoon (*Source 6*).
2 Work in pairs and tell each other what impression Cecil Rhodes leaves on you.
3 What message is the cartoonist trying to get across?

Views on Africa:
1 *Sources 7–9* illustrate what the European colonists thought of themselves and of the natives in the colonies.
  a Note their views under the following headings:

How the Europeans see themselves	How they see the natives

  b Consult the glossary on the ideas of Social Darwinism (→) and compare the different views.
2 Find similarities between the message of the cartoon and the views expressed in *Sources 7–9*.

SOURCE 6:
"The Rhodes' Colossus"
(Cartoon of Cecil Rhodes, Punch 1892)

I say that we are the finest race in the world and that the more of the world we inhabit the better it is for the human race. Just imagine what change there would be if those parts that are at present inhabited by the most inferior human beings were brought under Anglo-Saxon influence. Think of the extra employment a new country added to our dominions would give. [...] The acquisition of the greater part of the world under our rule would simply mean an end to all wars. [...] Africa is lying ready for us, it is our duty to take it.

SOURCE 7: An excerpt from Cecil Rhodes' "Confession of Faith", 1877, abridged and simplified

[...] I say that in almost every country that has come under the rule of the Queen, [...] there has come with it a great improvement in the conditions of the majority of the population. No doubt when these conquests were made there was loss of life among the native populations. [...]
You cannot destroy the practices of barbarism, of slavery, of superstition without the use of force.

SOURCE 8: An excerpt from a speech by Joseph Chamberlain, 31 March 1897 (abridged and simplified)

There is a struggle of race against race and of nation against nation. Is it not a fact that [...] our colonies have been won by the ejection of inferior races [...]?
We find that the law of the survival of the fittest is that of the gregarious animal. The path of progress is strewn with the wrecks of nations.

SOURCE 9: Karl Pearson, a British professor of mathematics in 1900

▼▼▼

Source 7
• *dominion* [dəˈmɪnɪən] country ruled by another government
• *inferior* [ɪnˈfɪərɪə] lower in value or rank

Source 8
• *barbarism* [ˈbɑːbərɪzəm] the lack of laws, manners, culture or civilisation
• *superstition* [ˌsuːpəˈstɪʃn] belief in magic powers

Source 9
• *ejection* [ɪˈdʒekʃn] throwing out with force
• *the fittest* the best, the strongest
• *gregarious* [grɪˈgeərɪəs] living in groups
• *(to) be strewn with* [struːn] be covered with

3 Techniques of expansion and conquest

Describing the cartoon
perspective
- in the backgound
- in the foreground
- pyramid ['pɪrəmɪd]

making assumptions
- (to) represent
- (to) stand for
- (to) illustrate
- (to) suggest
- (to) symbolize
- (to) refer to
- (to) relate to

describing the people
- smart
- top hat Zylinder(hut)
- fez [fez]
- (to) make/do a deal
- (to) bow [baʊ] bend your head or body forward to show respect
- (to) meet
- meeting
- (to) accept
- (to) hand over give sth. to sb.
- (to) be involved in

describing the lion
- key
- paw [pɔː] foot of an animal
- slip of paper small piece of paper
- king
- majestic [məˈdʒestɪk] having or showing majesty, grand
- imposing impressive in appearance
- (to) guard keep sb. or sth. safe from others

▼▼▼

Source 1
- loan money lent to sb.
- investment money used to make profit
- share Aktie
- (to) purchase buy
- lion's share the biggest part (of the profit)

Source 2
- merchant man merchant ship
- squadron military unit consisting of 10 to 18 people
- breakwater barrier to break the force of the sea

3.1 The Suez Canal

SOURCE 1: Punch cartoon of 1876, commenting on the British acquisition of large numbers of shares in the Suez Canal

Opening up Egypt:

1 Read the entry on the Suez Canal (→). Then look at *Source 5* on p. 66. Why was the Suez Canal so important for the British?
2 Describe the cartoon *(Source 1)*. The words on the left will help you.
3 What does the lion in *Source 1* represent? Explain how the cartoonist signals that this nation has got "the lion's share"?
4 How was the plan carried out? Consider the different parties involved and the military means.
5 Study the way the correspondent presents the preparations and the attack in *Sources 2–3*.

In June 1882 Egyptian nationalists organised anti-foreign riots in Alexandria, during which some Europeans lost their lives. Gladstone, the British Prime Minister, ordered his army to attack Alexandria. After the invasion of the country, the Egyptian rebel forces were defeated at the battle of Tal-El-Kebir. Egypt was then made a British protectorate. Note that since 1820 Alexandria's harbour had been connected with the River Nile by way of the Mahmudija Canal.

From our correspondent, Alexandria, 10 July, 12.30 p.m.

Everything seems to be ready for immediate action. [...] I'm writing this on board *Helicon*, four miles to the north of Pharos point [...]. All the ships left the harbour this morning, except the *Invincible*, *Monarch*, *Bittern* and *Beacon*, and a few merchant men who were hurriedly preparing to get under way.

The whole French Squadron steamed out to sea between 8 and 9 o'clock this morning, and the ships anchored about two miles outside the breakwater. The American, Austrian, Russian and Italian vessels of war have also anchored near them. [...]

SOURCE 2: *An excerpt from* The Times *of 11 July 1882*

Bombardments of the forts at Alexandria (noon)

The first shot was fired at Pharos Fort this morning at 7 o'clock by the *Alexandria*. About four minutes afterwards a general signal was hoisted by the *Invincible* to attack the enemy's batteries.

The signal was no sooner made than the *Invincible*, *Monarch* and *Penelope* immediately opened fire on the [...] batteries. [...]

The damage which has been inflicted on the forts is tremendous. In some places nothing but a heap of ruins is to be seen.

SOURCE 3: *An excerpt from* The Times *of 12 July 1882*

3.2 German colonial policy

Berlin – West African Conference

Hosts	Conference called by the German chancellor Otto von Bismarck at the invitation of Germany and France
Time	November 1884 – February 1885
Place	Berlin, the capital of the German Empire
Participants	Representatives from 14 countries
Causes	British and Portuguese distrust towards – Belgium and France: ambitions in the Congo – Germany: expansion in East Africa and the Cameroons – Quarrels between France and Italy over Tunis
Aims	to ease tensions between the European powers
Results	– Congo Free State now property of King Leopold II of Belgium – Germany's claim to Tanganyika accepted – Freedom of trade of all nations in the basin of the Congo – Freedom of navigation on the Congo and the Niger – Methods to prevent slave trade agreed on – Christian missionaries, scientists and explorers under special protection – Mutual information about new coastal possessions – Methods to protect existing rights on the coasts agreed on

A student's notes about the Berlin Conference

From notes to text:
① Let me start off by saying that … / To start with, the German Chancellor had…

② The conference lasted from…till / The conference was from … till …

③ The Chancellor had chosen Berlin as … / The Chancellor had invited … to …

④ The conference was attended by … / All in all there were … by …

⑤ The conference had become neccessary because … / One reason for such a conference was …

⑥ The aim of the conference can be defined as follows … The idea/purpose of the conference was …

⑦ The conference led to the following results … The members agreed on the following arrangements …

▼▼▼

Source 3
- *(to) hoist* [hɔɪst] lift
- *(to) inflict* cause
- *tremendous* [trɪˈmendəs] very big

- *(to) claim* [kleɪm] demand or request sth. because (one believes) it is one's right or property
- *(to) ease tension* make the relations between people, groups, etc. less strained
- *mutual* [ˈmjuːtʃʊəl] felt or done by each towards the other

Dividing up Africa:

1. From notes to text: Use the student's notes and describe the Berlin Conference in a coherent text. The clues ① – ⑦ will help you.
2. Which results are territorial, diplomatic or economic arrangements?
3. Discuss the strategy of the European powers.
   a. What did the Europeans gain in Africa?
   b. What did the Africans lose?
4. Do you think the arrangements between the European states will work?

SOURCE 4: Extract from a talk given by Otto von Bismarck in the German Reichstag after acquiring Angra Pequena, which later became German South West Africa, on 26 June 1884

Meine von Sr. Majestät dem Kaiser *gebilligte Absicht* ist, die Verantwortung für die *materielle Entwicklung* der Colonie ebenso wie ihr Entstehen der Tätigkeit und dem *Unternehmergeiste* unserer *seefahrenden* und *handeltreibenden* Mitbürger zu überlassen und weniger *in der Form der Annektierung* von überseeischen Provinzen an das Deutsche Reich vorzugehen, als in der Form von *Gewährung* von *Freibriefen* nach Gestalt der *Royal charters*, im Anschluss an die ruhmreiche Laufbahn, welche die englische Kaufmannschaft bei Gründung der ostindischen Compagnie zurückgelegt hat, und den Interessen der Kolonie zugleich *das Regieren* derselben *im Wesentlichen* zu überlassen und ihnen nur die Möglichkeit europäischer *Jurisdiction* für Europäer und desjenigen Schutzes zu gewähren, den wir ohne *stehende Garnisonen* dort leisten können. [...]
Unsere Absicht ist nicht Provinzen zu gründen, sondern kaufmännische Unternehmungen, *aber in der höchsten Entwicklung*, auch solche, die sich eine Souveränität, eine schließlich dem Deutschen Reich *lehnbar* bleibende, unter seiner *Protection* stehende kaufmännische Souveränität erwerben, *zu schützen* in ihrer freien Entwicklung sowohl gegen die Angriffe aus der unmittelbaren *Nachbarschaft* als auch gegen *Bedrückung und Schädigung von Seiten* anderer europäischer Mächte.

Summary of Contents
The Kaiser has agreed to Bismarck's intention of leaving the responsibility for the foundation and the economic development of the colonies to the enterprise of his seafaring and trading citizens. The Reich should not found colonies by annexing overseas territories.
Instead, colonies should be founded by granting charters modelled on the successful royal charters (→) granted to merchant traders of the English East India Company.
Basically, the administrators of the colonies should be left to their own devices. The Reich will only guarantee European jurisdiction for the Europeans and only such protection as is possible without the use of standing garrisons.
The Reich does not intend to found (overseas) provinces but intends to support merchant enterprises at their highest level. Their form of mercantile sovereignty will be politically dependent on the Reich and will be under its protection.
The intention of the Reich is to watch over the free development of the colonies as well as to safeguard them from the attacks of immediate neighbours as well as from the oppression and damage caused by other European powers.

▼▼▼
Source 5
- *kraal* [krɑːl] African village of huts
- *contract* treaty
- *pomp* ceremonial show
- *at random* without plan
- *mob* disorderly crowd of people
- *rumour* [ˈruːmə] talk, probably untrue
- *Mbusine* East African place name
- *grog* strong alcoholic drink
- *negotiations* diplomatic talks to reach an agreement
- *(to) maintain* keep up

When we were approaching a kraal where a contract was going to be made, I used to walk alongside my interpreter and with those of my people who could tell me something about the ruler in question, that is, about his character, his experiences in life, and about his property.
We walked more closely than on any other day, and when we entered the kraal, it was with much pomp and circumstance. If Arabs were near by who might have been enemies, I had my people fire their rifles at random to frighten the mob.
To look higher in rank than the Sultan, I had brought some flags with me, which I ordered to be hoisted at a suitable time and place. Moreover, I spread rumours about my power and influence. Finally, I had my hair cut short and, as I was also wearing my beard in a different fashion, I looked like an old respectable man.
When we entered the kraal, Jühlke and I would go to His Majesty and ask him – which otherwise never happened – if he allowed us to set up our camp. In Mbusine [...] we seated the Sultan between us [...] and put our arms around him from either side, then we had a glass of good grog with him and from the start we made His Majesty feel at ease. [...] Then we gave each other welcome presents, and we returned to our camp.
After lunch the Sultan paid his return visit where we made him drink sweet coffee. Then we started our negotiations [...] and entered into a contract. This done, the flags were hoisted on a [...] hilltop, the contract was read out in German by Dr. Jühlke, and I made a short speech and in this way took possession of the country. The ceremony ended with three cheers to the Kaiser and three salvos fired by us and our servants. This showed the blacks what to expect if the contract was broken.

SOURCE 5: How German East Africa came into being, an adapted and abridged excerpt from Carl Peter's report (1884)

German methods of colonial acquisition:
1 Read and compare the English and the German text in *Source 4*. Which English expressions correspond to those highlighted in the German text?
2 How does Bismarck see the role of the German government in *Source 4*?
3 Discuss Bismarck's concept of colonisation from a financial and political point of view.

A coloniser at work (*Source 5*):
1 Describe the picture Peters draws of himself and the Sultan.
2 Name and characterise the ways by which Peters established German rule?
3 Discuss the treaty from a moral point of view.

Warfare:
1 Compare the losses of the natives with those of the Germans (*Source 6*).
2 List Trotha's measures to end the war and explain the consequences (*Source 7*). The clues will help you.

1904–1907	year	1905–1907
Southwest Herero- and Nama rebellion	colony	East Africa Maji-Maji rebellion
about 67% Hereros (50–60,000) about 50% Nama (about 10,000) about 2,000 Germans	losses	at least 75,000 Africans (120,000 estimated)
585 mill. RM	costs	?

Even before 1900 some African peoples had seized arms to resist colonisation. Colonial wars were fought in many places in Africa. The harsh German rule in South-West Africa and in East Africa led to rebellions of native tribes.

SOURCE 6: The results of two big colonial wars

Clues	Text
South African tribe	Es fragte sich nun für mich, wie ist Krieg mit den Hereros zu beenden. […] Es wird möglich sein, durch die Besetzung der
waterholes	Wasserstellen […] und durch eine rege
army units	5 Beweglichkeit der Kolonnen die kleinen nach
retreating groups	Westen zuströmenden Teile des Volkes zu
(to) make repeated attacks	finden und sie allmählich aufzureiben. […] Da ich mit den Leuten weder paktieren kann
without the expressed instruction	noch ohne ausdrückliche Weisung seiner 10 Majestät des Kaisers und Königs will, so ist
rigorous treatment	eine gewisse rigorose Behandlung aller Teile der Nation notwendig. Ich habe gestern, vor meinem Abmarsch, die in den letzten Tagen
native warriors	ergriffenen Orlog-Leute kriegsgerichtlich court-martialled 15 verurteilt, aufhängen lassen und habe alle zugelaufenen Weiber und Kinder wieder in das Sandfeld unter Mitgabe der abgefaßten Proklamation an das Volk zurückgejagt. […] Sie müssen jetzt im Sandfeld untergehen oder
Botswana	20 über die Bechuanagrenze überzugehen (to) cross the border trachten. Dieser Aufstand ist und bleibt der
racial struggle	Anfang eines Rassenkampfes, den ich schon 1897 in meinen Berichten an den Reichskanzler vorausgesagt habe.

Hohenlohe-Schillingsfürst, Chlodwig, Fürst zu (Imperial Chancellor, 1894–1900)

SOURCE 7: Letter from von Trotha to the Generalstabschef von Schlieffen, 4 October 1904

4 Europeans in Africa

4.1 Germans in East Africa

SOURCE 1: Paying homage to the Kaiser

Talking about the cartoon
paying homage
- (to) submit to give in to sb. who has more power
- superior [suːˈpɪərɪə]
- inferior [ɪnˈfɪərɪə]
- native person born in a place or country and associated with it by birth
- traditional clothing
- uniform
- askari German trained African soldier
- humble [ˈhʌmbl] having a low or modest opinion of one's own importance
- servant person who works in sb.'s household for money
- offering sth. given as a gift or contribution
- spiked helmet Pickelhaube
- German Imperial Eagle deutscher Reichsadler

weapons
- rifle [ˈraɪfl]
- spear [spɪə]
- shield

mood
- joyful
- grateful

Source 1
- (to) pay homage to [ˈhɒmɪdʒ] give respect to

Source 2
- sovereignty [ˈsɒvrəntɪ] supreme power
- amendment [əˈmendmənt] minor change or addition to a document
- (to) absorb [əbˈsɔːb] take in
- (to) merge [mɜːdʒ] combine
- High Commissioner person who represents the crown
- (to) exercise use one's power
- chiefdom rule of a chief
- (to) retain not to take away
- (to) suit be good for

On February 27, 1885, the German Emperor William I placed Carl Peters' territorial gains in East Africa under his sovereignty and the control of his government.
The Emperor agreed to the treaties which had been made by Peters' colonising society*. These treaties granted jurisdiction to Peters' society between the African natives, the German settlers and traders, and people of non-German nationality. However, the Emperor did not rule out future amendments to his charter.
But the Emperor stated, Peters' colonising society should only be run by members of German nationality.

*Gesellschaft für deutsche Kolonisation

SOURCE 2: The Imperial Charter for Carl Peters (abridged, simplified and translated)

Understanding propaganda:
1 Describe the arrangement of people and objects in *Source 1*. Pay special attention to the position of the people. The words on the left may help you.
2 What message is the artist trying to get across?
3 Discuss the impression this picture may have left on a native and a German colonist.

German rule in East Africa:

1. Look at *Source 2*. Go through the text and note the institutions and people involved in the charter. Transfer your notes to a flow chart. Work with boxes and arrows. Write a key to the chart. The information on flow charts in the HISTORY SKILLS box on p. 47 may help you.
2. Imagine you were a member of Peters' colonising society. Name and discuss the pros and cons of the new status of the society.
3. How does the cartoonist in *Source 3* describe animal life in the jungle? The words on the right may help you.
4. What changes took place after the German take-over of African territories according to the two cartoons (*Source 3*)?
5. In what way does this cartoon (*Source 3*) show how the Europeans usually treated the African peoples?

4.2 The British colonies

British rule in Nigeria:

1. Read the notes below. Put them in a logical order. Consider the dates, the mention of Lugard's name as well as the description of British administration since 1912.
2. Draw Lugard's system in the form of a flow chart. The HISTORY SKILLS box on p. 47 may help you.
3. What were the advantages of this system to the British?

SOURCE 3: *Then and after: The system of colonising societies was reformed after several uprisings of native tribes (See Source 8 in Chapter 3) in the first decade of the 20th century. From then on, the German colonies were placed under the control of a special office, the so-called 'Kolonialamt' instituted by the 'Reichstag' and the 'Kanzler' to prevent further misrule and brutalities.*

Talking about the cartoons
animals
- elephant
- lion
- monkey
- bird
- snake
- giraffe [dʒɪˈrɑːf]
- crocodile [ˈkrɒkədaɪl]
- hippo [ˈhɪpəʊ]

vegetation
- jungle [ˈdʒʌŋɡl]
- waterfall
- palm-tree [ˈpɑːm triː]

order
- military ~
- (to) parade
- (to) stand in neat rows
- (to) present arms
- (to) goose-step march without bending the knees

a) In 1906 the colony of Lagos was absorbed into the southern protectorate and in 1914 the two protectorates were merged to form the largest British colony in Africa.

b) Frederick D. Lugard was sent to Nigeria, becoming High Commissioner in 1900, and by 1903 had occupied northern Nigeria.

c) The Royal Niger Company was taken over by the British Colonial Office and became the Niger Coast Protectorate in 1893.

d) Lugard served as Governor General in Nigeria (1912–1919). He developed the doctrine of indirect rule. He believed that the colonial administration should exercise its control through traditional native chiefdoms and institutions.

e) Following the conquest of the Kingdom of Benin, this became a protectorate of southern Nigeria in 1900.

f) Lugard's indirect administration retained the powers of the chiefs and emirs of its 150 or more tribes.

g) 'Indirect rule' was cheaper, more economical in men and less likely to provoke opposition than direct administration. In the north, systems of justice and taxation were reformed to suit the colonial regime.

Notes on British Rule in Nigeria

4.3 The French colonies

Home from school

I came home from school, threw my school bag down in the hall and shouted out like a town-crier:
"Bonjour, maman!"
In French.
She was standing there, rocking from one foot to the other, and looking at me through two round balls of tenderness: her eyes. She was so tiny, so fragile, that she would easily have fitted into my bag, between two schoolbooks illustrating science and civilization.
"Un sandwich", said my brother Nagib. "You cut some bread in half lengthwise and put maman between the two pieces. Ha ha! Of course, that wouldn't be very tasty. You'd have to put a whole packet of butter in, too. Ha ha!"
He worshipped his mother. He never married. 1m 80cm tall at the age of twelve, 2m 10cm as an adult. The power and the joy of eating and laughing, of getting up and going to bed with the sun.
"Listen to me, son", my mother said, reproachfully. "How often do I have to tell you to rinse your mouth out when you come home from school?"
"Every day, maman, every day the same. Apart from on Thursdays, Sundays and holidays. I'm going, maman."
"And do me a favour – take those pagan's clothes off."
"Oui, maman. Straight away."
"Go on, off you go, mon petit, concluded Nagib, clicking his fingers. Obey the 'Giver of Life'."
She ran after him, chasing him with a tea towel and he tried to escape, curving his back, terrorized, shrieking with laughter.
I went to clean my teeth with some toothpaste which she had made herself. Not for killing microbes with. She didn't know what they were – and neither did I, at the time (microbes, complexes, problems ...). But to get rid of the remains of the French language, which I had dared to use in her house, in front of her.
I took off my outdoor clothes and put on the ones which she had made and sewn for me herself.

SOURCE 4: An excerpt from La Civilisation, ma mère by Driss Chraïbi

Describing the photo
clothing ['kləʊðɪŋ]
• European ~
• traditional ~
• (to) cover the whole body
• long garments ['gɑːmənts] long articles of clothing
• burnous(e) [bɜːˈnuːs] long loose outer garment with sleeves and a hood worn in many Arab and Maghreb countries by men
• headscarf material tied round the head, worn instead of a hat
• trousers
• school uniform

Source 4
• bonjour hallo
• tenderness feeling of affection and love for sb.
• fragile ['frædʒaɪl] weak, easy to hurt
• lengthwise der Länge nach
• (to) worship love and respect
• reproachfully vorwurfsvoll
• Thursdays (formerly, in France) a day without school and reserved for the private study of religion

SOURCE 5: Street scene in Marrakesh

Between tradition and assimilation:

1. Go through the text (Source 4) and concentrate on the narrator and his brother Nagib. Note down all the information about language, clothes, and schooling.
2. Giving up your mother tongue and traditional clothes must be more than just giving up words or articles of clothing. How is this shown in the reaction of the narrator's mother? Look for clues and comment on them.
3. What experiences in a colonised society might have shaped the different reactions of these three Moroccans? Look at the map on p. 81 and name other African countries which could have a similar French heritage.
4. Describe the photo (Source 5). How does it reflect the situation described in the story? The words on the left may help you.

4.4 The economy of the colonies

SOURCE 6: German cartoon "So kolonisiert der Engländer!"

... Especially in the Tabora and Muanza district, the Blacks are filled with terrible hatred towards the Europeans on the stations.

The main reason for this is the so-called head- or hut-tax [Kopf- oder Hüttensteuer]. The Negroes can hardly ever sell the products of their fields at a
5 *profit. They have to deliver almost all their cattle and goats in order to pay the (usual) tax and only very few have still got some livestock of their own. Anyone who can't pay the tax has to work for the station far away from his people and is at the mercy of the askaris who follow him with a sjambok.*

The Negro is filled with extreme hatred for the so-called tribute work
10 *[Tributarbeit], the duration of which is not properly controlled. However, he has to submit to it, otherwise his livestock will be taken away from him, or his hut and all his belongings will be burnt.*

(A German decree of 1905 also made it possible to force native African males to maintain public roads without payment.)

SOURCE 7: Extract from a report by Walter Liebinger. (He was a settler in German East-Africa. His report is from 3 October 1905.)

A German view of British colonialism:
1. Describe the activities of the three Englishmen in *Source 6*.
2. What role within the colonial economy has the cartoonist given each of them?
3. How do you think a contemporary British nationalist might have reacted to this German cartoon?

The German way of making profit:
1. If Liebinger's report (*Source 6*) is correct, what role did the Africans play in the economy of the colony?
2. Talk about the similarities between the message of the cartoon and Liebinger's observations. The words on the right may help you.
3. Look at *Source 8*. How do you think the European colonists on their stations (as described in *Source 7*) profited from the system of tribute work?

Comparing sources
exploitation
- (to) exploit sb. [ɪkˈsplɔɪt] use sb. selfishly and unfairly for one's own profit or advantage
- (to) manipulate [məˈnɪpjʊleɪt] control or influence sb. by unfair means
- (to) maltreat [ˌmælˈtriːt] treat sb. badly or cruelly
- (to) squeeze sth. out of sb. get sth. from sb. through pressure
- (to) work sb. to death make sb. work so hard that it kills them
- hard labour very hard and difficult work

religion
- religious rite [raɪt] Ritus
- last rites duty performed by a priest before you die

▼▼▼

Source 6
- *pressing board* Preßbalken
- *capstan* Drehkreuz, Presse
- *bible* Bibel
- *prayer book* Gebetbuch
- *clergyman* man of the church

Source 7
- *station* large farm owned by Europeans with buildings, land, etc.
- *(to) deliver* hand over
- *livestock* animals kept on a farm
- *askari* native soldier in German service
- *duration* time-span
- *(to) submit* obey
- *belongings* property
- *sjambok* [ˈʃæmbɒk] Nilpferdpeitsche

Imperialism

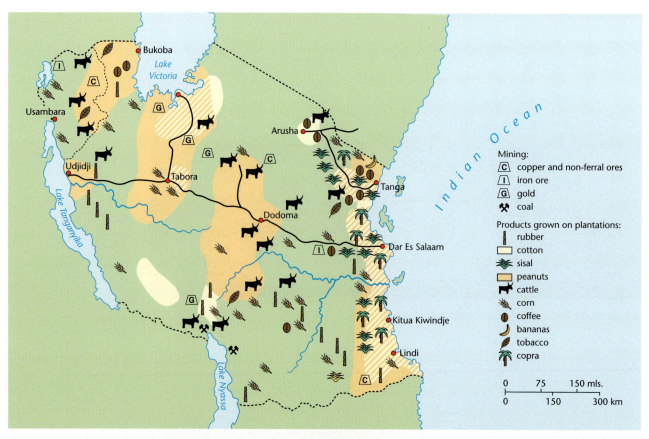

SOURCE 8: Economic map of German East Africa

	1894	1900	1906	1912
Sisal	...	0.02	1.37	7.36
Rubber	0.61	1.06	2.39	8.43
Hides, Furs	0.02	0.10	2.03	4.07
Cotton	...	...	0.18	2.11
Copra	0.17	0.21	1.09	1.57
Coffee	...	0.28	0.53	1.90
Ivory	2.15	1.00	0.43	0.36
Total export	**4.88**	**4.29**	**11.00**	**31.42**

SOURCE 9: Exports from German East Africa in million RM (Imperial Marks)

Source 8
- *sisal* ['saɪsl] tropical plant (Sisalagave)
- *copra* ['kɒprə] dried coconut, from which oil is extracted to make soap etc.

Source 9
- *hides* Häute
- *furs* Felle
- *ivory* Elfenbein
- *cash-crops* profit-oriented crops

Source 12
- *partition* [pɑːˈtɪʃn] division, especially of a country, into two or more parts

Source 13
- *clove* [kləʊv] dried unopened flower-bud of the tropical myrtle tree, used as a spice (Gewürznelke)

Colony	Subsidies
South-West Africa	278 mill. RM
East Africa	122 mill. RM
Cameroon	48 mill. RM
Togo	3.5 mill. RM
Kiautschou	174 mill. RM
German New Guinea	19 mill. RM
Samoa	1.5 mill. RM

SOURCE 10: Imperial subsidies for the German colonies until 1914

Raw materials imported from the colonies as a proportion of total raw materials imported	1.6%
Colonies' share of German empire's exports	0.5%
Colonies' share of German empire's capital exported	2.0%
German settlers in the African colonies until 1913 as a proportion of all the emigrants from the German Reich 1871–1914	0.03%

SOURCE 11: The economic importance of the German colonies in 1913

	1. Total exports	2. Exports to tropical Africa	3. Total imports	4. Imports from tropical Africa
1877–1879	194,427	1,249	375,394	1,805
1898–1901	267,266	3,062	500,161	2,572

SOURCE 12: *British trade with tropical Africa before and after the partition (in £ 1000's as annual average)*

Trade with Africa:

1 Look at *Sources 8–9*. Consult an encyclopedia about the products which are mentioned.
   a What were the various products used for?
   b Where did the various plants originally come from?
2 Discuss the possible effects which the introduction of these colonial cash-crops had on:
   a the small East-African farmers, fishermen and cattle breeders,
   b the original African wildlife and plants,
   c the territories of the different tribes.

Profiting from Africa:

1 Look at *Sources 10–11*. How important was the colonial trade to Germany? The words on the right may help you.
2 Compare the economic importance of the colonies to the Germans with their importance to the British, by looking at the figures in *Sources 9–12*. The words on the right may help you.
3 Work out and compare
   a the ratio between total exports and exports to tropical Africa,
   b the ratio between total imports and imports from tropical Africa from 1877–1879 and from 1889–1901.
4 Contrast export and import figures to and from Africa from 1877–1879 and from 1898–1901 *(Source 12)*.

Post colonial trade:

1 Compare the list of products in *Sources 8–9* with those in *Source 13*.
2 Compare the exports in *Source 13* with the numbers in *Source 9*.

Major exports are (in the 1990s): coffee, cotton, sisal, cloves, tea, tobacco, cashew nuts and diamonds.

SOURCE 13: *Exports from Tanzania today*

Describing and analysing statistics

import ['ɪmpɔːt]
• (to) ~ [ɪm'pɔːt] bring in goods or ideas from another country

export ['ekspɔːt]
• (to) ~ [ek'spɔːt] send goods to another country for sale

import figures
amount/number/quantity of goods brought into a country

export figures
amount/number/quantity of goods sent to another country

increase
• (to) ~
• (to) go up
• (to) be up to …
• (to) rise to …
• (to) double
• (to) triple
• (to) quadruple

decrease
• (to) ~
• (to) go down to …
• (to) fall to …
• twofold
• threefold

movement of figures
• (to) grow at a rate of … %
• (to) fall at a rate of … %
• (to) amount to …
• (to) add up to …
• (to) be as much as in …
• (to) reach a peak of …
• (to) fall to a low of …
• from … to
• over a span of … years/days

comparing figures
• about
• around
• approximately

5 Colonial rivalries

5.1 The Fashoda Crisis

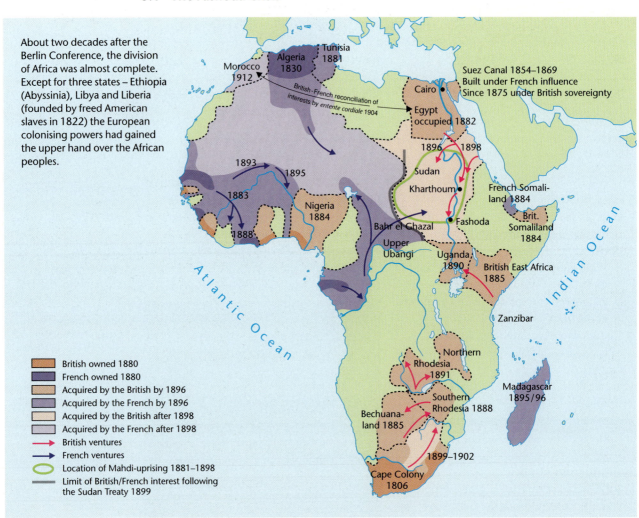

About two decades after the Berlin Conference, the division of Africa was almost complete. Except for three states – Ethiopia (Abyssinia), Libya and Liberia (founded by freed American slaves in 1822) the European colonising powers had gained the upper hand over the African peoples.

Legend:
- British owned 1880
- French owned 1880
- Acquired by the British by 1896
- Acquired by the French by 1896
- Acquired by the British after 1898
- Acquired by the French after 1898
- British ventures
- French ventures
- Location of Mahdi-uprising 1881–1898
- Limit of British/French interest following the Sudan Treaty 1899

SOURCE 1: British and French colonial policy in Africa

Fashoda Crisis, 1898. Fashoda is a settlement on the Upper Nile in the Sudan, now renamed Kodok. On 10 July 1898 a French expedition, led by Commander Marchand, reached Fashoda after a two-year trek across Africa from the French Congo. The expedition was sponsored by the French government. Since the British regarded the Upper Nile as part of their zone of influence, Marchand's presence was a clear challenge. Further north the British army under Kitchener was advancing southwards to reconquer the Sudan, which the Egyptians had abandoned thirteen years earlier. Kitchener, after the battle of Omdurman, moved to confront Marchand, and met him on 19 October 1898. Kitchener asked Marchand to withdraw, the French officer refused, and both men asked their governments to settle the dispute. 'We claim the Sudan by right of conquest', said the British Prime Minister Lord Salisbury (→). The British were in a stronger position than the French. They controlled Egypt, and their communications to Fashoda were secured. Marchand had a weak force of about 100 Senegalese soldiers; Kitchener had an army. The French failed to gain any diplomatic support from either Germany or Russia. For a time there was a possibility of war between the two countries. It was not until 3 November 1898 that the French admitted defeat and ordered Marchand to withdraw. Four months later, the French gave up all claims to the Nile valley, but were promised the lands west of the Nile not already under European occupation.

SOURCE 2: A handbook article

① place
② main agents
③ subject
④ chronology
⑤ main interests
⑥ military strength, position
⑦ results

There is no need to argue the point; if a householder finds a man in his back garden, he does not go to arbitration about the matter or enter into elaborate arguments to show that he, the householder, is the owner of that garden. He simply orders the trespasser out, and, if he will not go of his own accord, he has to go in another fashion.

SOURCE 3: Extract from The Evening News, 13 September 1898

We cannot conceal from ourselves that Lord Salisbury and his colleagues have taken a position from which retreat is impossible. One side or the other will have to give way; that side cannot, after the publication of these papers (official blue book, →), be Great Britain.

SOURCE 4: Extract from The Times, 10 October 1898

SOURCE 5: A British cartoon (The Duke of Wellington in the foreground (1769–1852) was the British General who defeated Napoleon at Waterloo in 1815 with the help of Prussian troops. Lord Salisbury, the British Prime Minister and foreign secretary, contrary to his government, wanted to steer a hard course.)

On the brink of war:
1 Find Fashoda on the map *(Source 1)*. Why was the town of Fashoda so important in the context of Britain's African colonies?
2 What policy did France pursue in Africa *(Source 1)*?
3 Look at *Source 2*. Study the text and make notes following the clues ① – ⑦.
4 Explain why the British gained the upper hand in the Fashoda Crisis *(Source 2)*.
5 Explain the position the newspaper articles take in the conflict *(Sources 3–4)*.
6 Compare the extract from the *Evening News* with that from the *Times (Sources 3–4)*. Which of the two 'voices' is more nationalistic? Why?

Making fun of national symbols:
1 How does the cartoonist describe the position of the French at Fashoda? And of the British?
2 For the French the 'cock' is a national symbol which became popular during the French Revolution, with 'gallus' meaning both 'cock' and 'Gaul' (to denote a Frenchman). Especially in times of war or national crisis, the bird symbolizes the readiness of the French people to defend the interests of their nation. Look at the clues in *Source 5* again. Discuss the possible effect of this cartoon on a French nationalist.
3 Here are some more animals which are still used as national symbols: the eagle, the lion, the elephant, the rhino; why do states use animals as national symbols? Consider their qualities.

Source 2
• *trek* journey
• *(to) sponsor* give money to
• *zone of influence* an area which a nation claims
• *challenge* provocation
• *(to) abandon* [əˈbændən] give up
• *(to) withdraw* go back
• *(to) settle the dispute* end the quarrel
• *(to) be secured* be safe
• *(to) fail* not succeed

Source 3
• *(to) go to arbitration* decide who is right or wrong
• *elaborate* [ɪˈlæbərət] worked out with great care
• *of his own accord* voluntarily

Source 4
• *(to) conceal from* hide
• *(to) retreat* withdraw

5.2 The Kaiser and the Boer War

When gold was found in the Boer republic of the Transvaal in southern Africa (1884 onward), the Boers, the descendants of earlier Dutch farmers in the Cape, tried to restrict the influence of the new immigrants on their country, which the British, however, regarded as part of the Empire.

Cecil Rhodes (→), Prime Minister of the Cape Colony, tried to remove the president of the Transvaal Republic, Paul 'Oom' Kruger, in 1895 by encouraging a military raid on the territories of the Boers.

Having successfully beaten off the British, President Kruger received a telegram from the German Kaiser, William II (1896). For a moment the Kaiser had even thought of sending troops from East Africa to protect the 15,000 Germans in the Transvaal and of establishing a German protectorate.

SOURCE 6: *The background to the Kruger telegram*

Telegramm Kaiser Wilhelm II. an den Präsidenten Krüger vom 3. Januar 1896
Ich spreche Ihnen meinen aufrichtigsten Glückwunsch aus, dass es Ihnen, ohne an die Hilfe befreundeter Mächte zu appelieren, mit Ihrem Volke gelungen ist, in eigener Tatkraft gegenüber den bewaffneten Scharen, welche als Friedensstörer in Ihr Land eingedrungen sind, den Frieden wiederherzustellen und die Unabhängigkeit des Landes gegen Angriffe von außen zu wahren.

I express my sincere congratulations to you that, supported by your people, and without appealing for the help of friendly powers, you have succeeded by your own energetic action against armed bands which invaded your country as disturbers of peace, and have thus been able to restore peace, and safeguard the independence of the country against attacks from outside. – William, I.R. (Imperator Rex – this Latin phrase stands for the sender's title, 'Emperor and King')

SOURCE 7: *The Kaiser's telegram to President Kruger, 3 January 1896*

SOURCE 8: *Making fun of a rival*

Talking about colonial policies
friendship
- (to) win sb.'s ~
- (to) seek ~ with sb.
- (to) make friends with sb.
- (to) get on well with sb.

agreement
- (to) agree with sb.
- (to) pull sb. over to sb.'s side
- (to) support sb.'s efforts
- (to) sympathize with sb. ['sɪmpəθaɪz]

disagreement
- (to) disagree with sb.
- (to) be against sth.
- (to) restrict sb.'s power
- (to) curb sb.'s influence
- (to) exclude sb. from sth.
- (to) be afraid of sb./sth.
- (to) fall out with sb.

competition [ˌkɒmpə'tɪʃn]
- competitor [kəm'petɪtə]
- rival ['raɪvl]

▼▼▼

Source 7
- *thus* so, in this way

Source 8
- *(to) sweep* fegen
- *(to) drive out* lahmlegen

Source 9
- *scheme* plot
- *(to) cruise* make a journey by sea

Challenging a rival:

1. Read the English version of the telegram (Sources 6–7). Look at the highlighted expressions and find the German equivalents in the German text.
2. Which part of the telegram must have made the British particularly angry? Why?
3. Imagine you were one of the Kaiser's political advisers. Stage a role-play in which you try to prevent the German Emperor from sending the telegram. Consider the view Bismarck expressed at the Berlin Conference in 1884/85 and the military strength of Britain as shown in Egypt and the Sudan.
4. Consult the map of South Africa and identify Mafeking, Kimberley and Ladysmith.
5. How does the German cartoon (Source 8) present the British military? Discuss the provocation.
6. 'John Bull' (→) is the historical nickname of the English nation. Do you know the nicknames for some other nations? In what context do you think are they 'safe' to use?

5.3 The first and second Moroccan Crises (1905–1911)

The Sudan (Fashoda) and the Transvaal (South Africa) were not the only trouble spots which led to conflicts between rival colonial powers.
Britain = B, France = F, Germany = G, Morocco = M, German emperor = K

- 1904 – skilful French diplomacy: B and F agree on the *entente cordiale* (friendly agreement), its main points: colonial matters (F pro B, chief influence; B supports F in Morocco)
  – K fears Franco-British scheme?
  – F against G influence in North Africa?
- 1905 – K: mediterranean cruise, in Tangier fierce speech of K, demands conference on independent M, warning to F
- 1906 – Algeciras (town): conference held, participants: B, Italy, Russia, Spain, USA, support for F, M = still independent, but F main power in M
- 1911 – 2nd crisis: rebel forces, sultan of M trapped, military invention by F
  – K sends gunboat *Panther* to Agadir to protect G business interests
  – B backs F's position and threatens with war, compromise after negotiations: G getting 100,000 sq miles of French Congo north of the Cameroons
  – M: protectorate of F, Tangier: Spanish M, Italy: Tripolitania (between Tunisia and Egypt)

SOURCE 9: Notes about conflicts between rival colonial powers

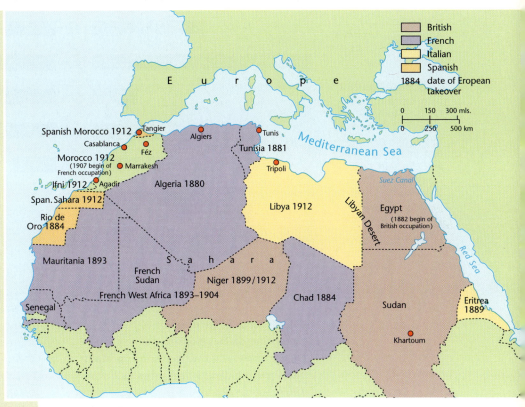

SOURCE 10: Identifying interests

Alliance and isolation:

1. Read the notes in *Source 9* carefully. Then write out the information given there in full sentences. The words on the left will help you.
2. Locate Tangier on the map (Source 10) and discuss its strategic importance as a naval base in Africa.
3. Sum up the development of the two crises over Morocco.
4. Retrace the conflict from either a German or a French perspective.

5.4 On the brink of war: The arms race

At the turn of the century, colonial rivalries began to cast political shadows on the relationship between the individual colonial powers. As a result of the Fashoda incident, Britain decided to give up her policy of 'splendid isolation'(→). In 1898, encouraged by an enthusiastic Kaiser and the 'Naval League' (Flottenverein →), Admiral von Tirpitz (→) began to launch an ambitious naval construction programme (Flottenbauprogramm). It was the two Moroccan Crises and Germany's refusal to accept disarmament proposals at the Second Convention of the Hague in 1907, which made Britain move even closer to France.

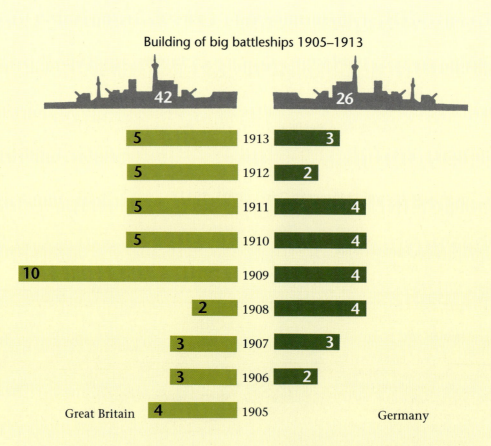

SOURCE 11: Construction of big battle ships

The Arms' Race in Europe – commenting on developments:

1. Draw a time line showing all the important dates and incidents in the arms race until 1907 (Source 11).
2. Draw a line graph illustrating the individual naval programmes. Use different colours.
3. Talk about the development from a British point of view. (Consult *chapter 1, Source 4*)
4. Connect the data and the text of *Source 11* with the political events as outlined in *chapter 5*.
5. Look at *Source 12* and identify the two men. What's the message of the cartoon?
6. Find out how the European alliance systems changed between 1871 and 1914. Pay special attention to the following terms: Dreikaiserbund, Triple Alliance, Dual Alliance.

Between 1908 and 1912, further attempts at solving the naval question between Britain and Germany failed. Instead, the German Chancellor von Bülow came forward with new concepts to increase Germany's naval power. Finally, the British and French agreed on a military burden-sharing in case of a German naval attack and prepared for a special placing (disposition) of their navies in the Channel and the Mediterranean Sea.

Imperialism

Viewpoints on naval policy:
1. Why does von Tirpitz want a strong fleet for Germany *(Sources 13–14)*?
2. How did a high circulation paper such as the *Daily Mail (Source 15)* see von Tirpitz's maritime plans?
3. Read *Source 15* from von Tirpitz's point of view and comment.
4. 'Want of space at home' – Consult an encyclopaedia about Thomas Robert Malthus and his influence on 19th century political thought.

SOURCE 12: *How are we going to shake hands?*

> In my view, Germany will, in the coming century, rapidly drop from her position as a great power unless we begin to develop our maritime interests energetically, systematically and without delay.

SOURCE 13: *German Admiral von Tirpitz on Germany's future in 1895*

> Under the present circumstances there is only one means to protect Germany's trade and colonies: Germany must have a fleet of such strength that in a war even the biggest fleet would run the risk of endangering its own superiority. For this purpose, it is not absolutely necessary that the German fleet is as big as the biggest naval power, because as a rule a big naval power will be unable to concentrate its whole force against us.

SOURCE 14: *Admiral von Tirpitz in 1900*

> While great naval power in the hands of Britain cannot constitute a menace, in the hands of Germany it will be a great peril to the world, the more so as the recent history of German policy is one of daring aggression and as the want of space at home compels Germany to conquer the colonies of others or perish.

SOURCE 15: *Daily Mail, 5 February 1903 on the German fleet under von Tirpitz's leadership*

▼▼▼

Source 11
- *ambitious* ehrgeizig
- *disarmament proposal* Abrüstungsvorschlag
- *The Hague* the government seat of the Netherlands
- *battleship* Schlachtschiff

Source 13
- *delay* time lost by inaction

Source 14
- *circumstance* ['sɜːkəmstəns] situation connected with an event or action
- *superiority* [suːˌpɪərɪˈɒrətɪ] the feeling of being better and stronger

Source 15
- *(to) constitute* ['kɒnstɪtjuːt] form
- *menace* ['menəs] threat
- *peril* great danger

6 Images and views of Africa

SOURCE 1: A European travelling in Africa, c. 1885

SOURCE 2: Carl Peters in Africa, c. 1890

SOURCE 3: Tourists in Africa, c. 1990

European views of Africa:
1. Look at *Sources 1–3*. Talk about age, gender and clothing of the Africans in these pictures. The words on the left will help you.
2. What functions are given to the Africans?
3. In what other roles are Africans often shown in European magazines and advertisements?
4. Compare these images with those presented by TV newscasts.
5. How does Sir Robertson see white rule in Africa? (*Source 4*)

Describing the photos
Europeans
- European clothes
- suit [suːt] a jacket and trousers (or skirt) that you wear together and that are made from the same material
- smart chic; well-dressed, neat and tidy
- white trousers
- sun-hat
- arrogant ['ærəgənt]
- pompous ['pɒmpəs]
- lazy ['leɪzɪ]
- cart [kɑːt] vehicle with two or four wheels used for carrying sth./sb.
- canopy ['kænəpɪ] cover which can be used as a shelter
- hammock ['hæmək] bed made of canvas or rope held up at each end

Africans
- native ['neɪtɪv] person who was born in a place
- barefoot ['beəfʊt] not wearing any shoes or socks
- naked ['neɪkɪd] not wearing any clothes
- half-naked
- dry
- dusty road
- (to) carry sth./sb.
- (to) beg ask for food or money because of one's poverty

I think a great deal is now spoken by people who don't know very much about the background to our rule in Africa. When we took over these countries there was very little government, there was very little civilisation, there was a great deal of inter-tribal warfare. Our policy in these countries was to impose ways of peace, and that's what we did. And we developed them as best we could. One thing that our critics seem to forget is that we had no money. The British government gave us nothing for many, many years. In the Sudan, there were no hospitals, there was no sort of modern government with ministries or anything of that kind. And when we left the Sudan there was a system of railways, there was a system of roads, there were schools, there was even a university. This was all done in the space of about fifty-eight years – and you could walk from one end of the Sudan to the other more safely than you could walk in the back streets of London, without any fear or danger. We had set up a civilisation that had not existed before.

SOURCE 4: Sir James Robertson, former Governor General of Nigeria on BBC 4, 1979

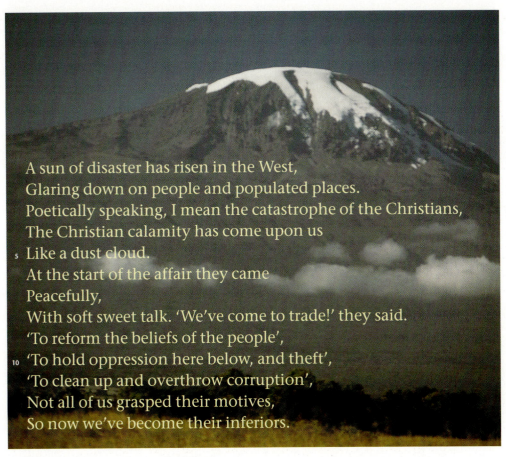

A sun of disaster has risen in the West,
Glaring down on people and populated places.
Poetically speaking, I mean the catastrophe of the Christians,
The Christian calamity has come upon us
5 Like a dust cloud.
At the start of the affair they came
Peacefully,
With soft sweet talk. 'We've come to trade!' they said.
'To reform the beliefs of the people',
10 'To hold oppression here below, and theft',
'To clean up and overthrow corruption',
Not all of us grasped their motives,
So now we've become their inferiors.

SOURCE 5: *An Arabic poem, written in 1900*

Through force, fraud and violence, the people of North, East, West, Central and Southern Africa were relieved of their political and economic power and forced to pay allegiance to foreign monarchs.
5 By means of unequal treaties the conquered countries were transformed into profitable fields for the investment of foreign capital. The economic wealth and resources of these colonies were exploited by and turned over to the imperialist powers, not in the interest of the
10 indigenous populations, but for the benefit of the metropolitan people. ... To the people of Asia and Africa imperialism meant, and still means, the exploitation of the mineral and agricultural wealth of their countries by foreign powers without their consent and without
15 compensation.

SOURCE 6: *Nelson Mandela on imperialism*

The oneness of community, for instance, is at the heart of our culture. The easiness with which Africans communicate with each other is not forced by authority but 5 is inherent in the make-up of African people. Thus, whereas the white family can stay in an area without knowing its neighbours, Africans develop a sense of be- 10 longing to the community within a short time of coming together. Many a hospital official has been confounded by the practice of Indians who bring gifts and pre- 15 sents to patients whose names they can hardly recall. Again, this is a manifestation of the inter-relationship between man and man in the black world, as opposed 20 to the highly impersonal world in which Whitey lives. These are characteristics we must not allow ourselves to lose. Their value can only be appreciated by those of us 25 who have not as yet been made slaves to technology and the machine.

SOURCE 7: *Stephen Biko on indigenous African cultures*

▼▼▼

Source 4
• *intertribal warfare* war between tribes
• *(to) impose* auferlegen

Source 5
• *disaster* sudden great misfortune
• *(to) glare* look angrily
• *calamity* cause that produces great evil, e.g. war
• *(to) halt* stop
• *theft* act of stealing
• *corruption* immorality; dishonestness
• *(to) grasp* understand sth.

Source 6
• *fraud* dishonest deals, false promises
• *(to) relieve* take away
• *(to) pay allegiance to* promise to be loyal to
• *indigenous* native
• *metropolitan people* inhabitants of the World's major cities
• *consent* permission

Source 7
• *oneness* being one, forming a coherent group
• *inherent* being a natural part of
• *make-up* character
• *(to) confound* confuse and surprise
• *manifestation* a clear sign/expression of

African voices:
1 What picture of European rule does the African poet draw *(Source 5)*? What words sum it up best?
2 How do Mandela's words *(Source 6)* support the poet's view?
3 Contrast Stephen Biko's text *(Source 7)* with Sir Robertson's thoughts *(Source 4)*.

15th

1492 Columbus lands in the new world

16th

1513 The Spaniard Juan Ponce de León lands in Florida
1534–1541 Voyages of the Frenchman Jacques Cartier along the St. Lawrence River in Canada
1584 Sir Walter Raleigh establishes the colony of Virginia at Roanoke Island

17th

1607 Founding of the Jamestown colony, Virginia
1612 Beginning of the cultivation of tobacco
1619 Arrival of the first African slaves in Virginia
1620 Arrival of the Pilgrims
1681 Charter of Pennsylvania granted to William Penn

18th

1733 Founding of Georgia, the last of the 13 English colonies
1755–1763 The French and Indian War, the American phase of the Seven Years war
1763–1765 British Prime Minister George Grenville pushes legislation through Parliament to tax the colonies directly
1764 Sugar Act
1765 Stamp Act
1766 Repeal of the Stamp Act
1767 Townshend Acts; Boston town meeting adopts non-importation agreement
1770 The Boston Massacre
1773 Boston Tea Party
1775–1783 War of Independence
1775 George Washington is appointed commander-in-chief of the American forces
1776 Declaration of Independence adopted
1777 Battle of Saratoga
1778 France signs Treaties of Commerce and Alliance with the United States
1780 Pennsylvania outlaws slavery
1783 Treaty of Peace between Great Britain and the United States, recognizing the latter's independence, is signed in Paris.

1719 Daniel Defoe (1660–1731) writes Robinson Crusoe
1726 Jonathan Swift (1667–1745) writes Gulliver's Travels
1735 Kay's Flying Shuttle Coke, Darby
mid-18th century: remarkable population increase
mid-18th century: closed field system, Norfolk Four-Course-Rotation system
1792–1860 Robert Blincoe

19th

1809–1882 Charles Darwin
1807 Luddite risings steam ship
1812 Luddite risings
1814 first locomotive built by Stephenson
1830 first railway Liverpool-Manchester Formation of the National Association for the Protection of Labour marks the beginning of the trade union movement
1832 first Parliamentary Reform
1837–1901 Queen Victoria

20th century

1756–1763 Seven Years' War between Britain and France
1757–1761 Robert Clive secures British dominion over India
1771 Duke of Bridgewater has canal built from Worsley to Manchester
1775 Watt's steam engine
1779 Spinning Mule, Spinning Jenny, Crompton
1786 power loom, Cartwright
1798 Dr Jenner – smallpox vaccine

1837–1839 Charles Dickens writes Oliver Twist
1847 Dr Simpson – chloroform used as anaesthetic
1848 Chartist's claims rejected
1851 The Great Exhibition, London
1858 Brunel's Great Eastern
1868 first Trade Union Congress
1893 Foundation of Independent Labour Party

1859–1869 Construction of the Suez Canal by the French engineer Ferdinand de Lesseps
1875 Britain's purchase of shares in the Suez Canal Company under Benjamin Disraeli
1877 Cecil Rhodes' Confession of Faith
1882 Bombardments of the forts of Alexandria; occupation of Egypt by the British
1884–1885 Otto von Bismarck's Berlin West Africa Conference
1884 Foundation of the Society for German Colonization by Carl Peters; Establishment of German South West Africa as a protectorate (Schutzgebiet) of the German Empire
1885 Establishment of German East Africa as a protectorate of the German Empire
1886 Foundation of the British Royal Niger Company
1893 Establishment of the Niger Coast Protectorate by the British Colonial Office
1896 Kaiser Wilhelm II's famous telegram of congratulation to President Paul Kruger of the South African Republic (Transvaal)
1899–1902 (Second) Anglo-Boer War
1898 Fashoda Crisis between Britain and France; Britain's abandonment of her policy of 'splendid isolation'
1898 Tirpitz' naval construction programme, designed to rival Britain's naval power

1904–1907/8 Herero Wars in German South West Africa
1905–1911 The First and Second Moroccan Crises
1912–1919 Frederick D. Lugard governor-general in Nigeria (doctrine of indirect rule)

Map of the world

Map of the world

Extra reading list

The Bride Price (Buchi Emechata)
OXFORD UNIVERSITY PRESS   76 342

When her father dies, Aku-nna and her young brother have no-one to look after them. They are welcomed by their uncle because of Aku-nna's 'bride price' – the money that her future husband will pay for her. In her new, strange home, one man is kind to her and teaches her to become a woman. The more the world tries to separate them, the more they are drawn together – until, finally, something has to break.

Britain and America – Tradition and Change
CORNELSEN   54 870

A selection of 136 texts which do justice not only to the history of the two countries, but to the social and political changes of recent years, too. The 12 chapters are arranged thematically. Four deal with Britain, four with the USA, and the remaining four with more general topics, of relevance to other industrialized nations too.

A Christmas Carol (Charles Dickens)
OXFORD ULIVERSITY PRESS   106 225

The most famous of Dickens' popular Christmas stories. The greedy, mean, old Scrooge is visited by his former business partner, who has been dead for seven years. He warns Scrooge that he will be haunted by three ghosts: *The Ghost of Christmas Present, The Ghost of Christmas Past,* and *The Ghost of Christmas Yet To Come*. They show him some scenes from his past, reveal to the old man the suffering he has caused, and what the consequences might be if he does not change his ways …

Cry Freedom (John Briley)
OXFORD UNIVERSITY PRESS   76 350

They said Steve Biko was a man of violence; then why did he talk of peace? They said he wanted revolution; so why did he talk of friendship? They said he died of hunger; why was his body broken and bruised? The story of a man's fight with apartheid and the former government of South Africa.

David Copperfield (Charles Dickens)
OXFORD UNIVERSITY PRESS   56 473

David Copperfield is a writer. In describing the ups and downs of his youth, some of it modelled on Dickens' own suffering as a boy, he paints a picture of 19th century English society. The novel shows how David learns from his experiences and, after a first un- happy marriage, finds happiness with a girl he has known since childhood. Dickens described the book as his own "favourite child".

Great Expectations (Charles Dickens)
OXFORD UNIVERSITY PRESS   106 420

The story of the young orphan boy, Pip, who unexpectedly becomes rich. But life in 19th century London as a wealthy gentleman has its drawbacks too – especially when you are in love with someone who does not love you. This is a story with a melodramatic plot, containing many comic characters.

Heat and Dust (Ruth Prawer Jhabvala)
OXFORD UNIVERSITY PRESS   100 740

These simple words describe the Indian summer. Everyone who experiences this heat and dust is changed forever. Here we see that, whether we look back sixty years or a hundred and sixty, it is not things that change, but people. And, in the heat and dust of an Indian summer, even people are not very different after all.

India – Old and New (Shahana Dasgupta)
CORNELSEN   51 528

India – many Europeans probably associate "a huge population", "starving people", "Taj Mahal" and "Gandhi" with it. But how does an Indian see her own country? A native author offers an unusual and highly informative picture of India's past and present.

Introducing New English Literatures
CORNELSEN   668 301

The English language belongs not only to the British and the Americans, but also to millions of other people throughout the five continents. And these people, of course, have their own literatures through which they express their culture and identity. A collection of stories from Australia, Canada, the Caribbean, India, New Zealand, Nigeria and South Africa.

Jane Eyre (Charlotte Brontë)
OXFORD UNIVERSITY PRESS   101 991

One of the classic love stories of all time. Jane goes to Thornfield Hall as a governess and falls in love with Rochester, the master there. Their wedding is interrupted when it is revealed that he is already married, to a mad woman, and Jane leaves. She later returns to Thornfield Hall to find it burnt out and Rochester blind and deformed. But now that his wife is dead, there is no longer any obstacle to their love.

King in a Cage (J. J. Graves)
CORNELSEN   69 737

When gold is discovered in the one small area of South Africa which has not been conquered by the British, Joseph Sharpton, the richest man in Africa, stops at nothing to get his hands on the land. He also decides that Edwina Sweet shall be his wife. How can she resist a man with so much wealth and power? Can Edwina escape him, or will she, like the rest of South Africa, come under his dominance?

The Land of their Fathers
(Allen J. Woppert)
CORNELSEN   68 030

The true story of the Ponca Indians, who went to court in 1879 to fight for the right to live on the "land of their fathers", instead of on a reservation. Will the Poncas be able to convince the court to recognize them as human beings too, with their own claim to US law?

Little Women (Louisa M. Alcott)
OXFORD UNIVERSITY PRESS   106 160

The popular story of four sisters, the daughters of an army chaplain, growing up in hard conditions in America in the 1860s. The story of their youth, childhood, marriages and support for one another, in spite of very different characters, takes place against the background of the American Civil War.

Oliver Twist (Charles Dickens)
OXFORD UNIVERSITY PRESS   106 276

The sordid reality of the London underworld in the 1830s. Young Oliver is born in a workhouse and later becomes involved with a gang of thieves in the London slums. After a brutal story including kidnapping, burglary, murder and several hangings, Oliver's true origins are revealed and he is adopted by a kindly gentleman.

"One Nation under God"
CORNELSEN   52 141

The USA is one of the most religious countries in the Western World: nine out of ten Americans say they believe in God. The influence of religion goes far beyond people's private lives, reaching into business, politics and the media. Religion is a major key to understanding American society – from the religious ideas of the American Indians, to Puritanism, to Televangelism.

Silas Marner (George Eliot)
OXFORD UNIVERSITY PRESS   107 590

An exciting story, full of humour and lively characters. The rich Silas has all his gold stolen by a good-for-nothing man whose brother, although in love with one woman, is secretly and shamefully married to another. They have a little girl, who runs away as her mother lies dying in the snow. She finds her way to Silas's cottage, where she brings him more happiness than his lost gold.

Student's Outline of British and American History
CORNELSEN 24 229
● ● ●

To understand political and cultural developments, it often helps to have a knowledge of the historical background against which they took place. This reference book covers the most important events in the two countries. Events are arranged chronologically and there are short essays in between, giving further information on significant epochs, problems and people.

The US Bill of Rights in Action
CORNELSEN 52 168
●

The first ten amendments to the US Constitution, known as the Bill of Rights, have safeguarded the rights and freedoms of American citizens for two centuries. To this day, the Supreme Court interprets these amendments and watches over their observance in a complex and constantly changing society.

USA A to Z (K. Carlson-Kreibohm)
CORNELSEN & OXFORD 31 870
●

An easy-to-use, alphabetical dictionary of terms covering a wide range of topics and trends, aspects of modern everyday society and their roots, giving the reader a broad overview of American life.

Victorian England
CORNELSEN 169 801
●

A collection of various Victorian documents, newspaper and magazine articles, reports, speeches, songs, pamphlets, literary texts, etc., commenting on the greatest changes ever to take place in the history of the modern world. These years of dramatic development upset the whole of Britain's social structure, causing mass poverty, slums and epidemic disease, yet they also transformed Queen Victoria's island into the leading power of the time.

The White House, Washington, D.C.
(K. Carlson-Kreibohm)
CORNELSEN 3 388
●

A lively, comprehensive look at the stages from politician to President of the United States, including primary election, party congress, election campaign, election and electoral college. The author describes the duties of a president, and gives us a glimpse behind the scenes of the White House.

● The American Revolution
● The Industrial Revolution
● Imperialism

If you would like to explore the topics covered in Spotlight on History, Volume 1 *further, you could consult the Cornelsen books used in your history lessons, too.*

Glossary

Allegiance (pledge of ~)
"I pledge allegiance to the flag of the United States of America and to the Republic for which it stands, one nation under God, indivisible, with liberty and justice for all." First said in 1892, under President Harrison, for patriotic exercise in schools to mark the 400th anniversary of the discovery of America. Original pledge written by Francis Bellamy. In 1954, the words "under God" were added.

Askari
German trained East-African soldier

Berlin West-Africa Conference
A series of negotiations in Berlin (Nov.1884 – Feb.1885) attended by the European great powers (Austria-Hungary, France, Germany, Great Britain, Italy and Russia), together with the United States and other European nations, to settle all matters concerning the Congo basin. It was called by the German chancellor, Bismarck, after Portugal, supported by Britain, objected to King Leopold II of Belgium's plans for colonizing the Congo. The result was the declaration that the whole Congo basin was neutral and that there was to be free trade and passage for all nations. It ended slave trade and led to the recognition of the independent Congo Free State.

Bill of Rights
The first ten amendments to the Constitution of the United States, which include a declaration of the fundamental rights of United States citizens. It became part of the Constitution in 1791.

Boston Gazette
Anti-British New England newspaper, founded in 1755. It was an immediate success in the colonies because of its support for American independence.

Botswana
Republic of Botswana, formerly **Bechuanaland**; country in Southern Africa bordered on the south by South Africa, on the north by Zambia. In 1884 it became the British Bechuanaland Protectorate and remained so until the late 1960s.

Campbell Soup Company
US manufacturer dating back to 1869. One of the largest manufacturers of canned foods, including the soups with the familiar red and white label.

Checks and balances
System of government brought in by the American Constitution writers. They were afraid of having too much power in one place, so they divided the government into three branches – the legislative branch (Congress) to make laws, the judicial branch (courts) to decide on the exact meanings of the laws, and the executive branch (the President, who is not a member of Congress) to oversee everything. Each branch has only limited powers and has ways of controlling the power of the other two branches, i.e. of "checking" and "balancing" it.

Child labour
The employment of children under a legal age. This was one of the serious problems of the early industrial era. Most countries now regulate child labour, which is a threat to the safety, health and education of children. Britain was the first country to use power machinery to spin and weave cotton, and it was there that children first worked in factories. Poor children, only seven and eight years old, were taken from the workhouses in the big towns to the mills in the north of England. Their new masters often treated them cruelly. They had little to eat and sometimes had to work for 18 hours a day. In 1819 the first law, which applied only to cotton mills, limited the working day to 12 hours and the age of workers to nine years or over. For the next 100 years, continual efforts were made to improve the child worker's lot.

Cholera
Infectious, often fatal disease with acute diarrhoea. With the increase of international trade and commerce in the 19th century, the disease found its way to western Europe, the first large epidemic being 1831–1832. The low standard of public and personal hygiene at that time gave it every chance of spreading.

Colony
Country or area settled, conquered or controlled by a more powerful country which uses the colony's resources in order to increase its own power or wealth.

Convention of the Hague (2nd ~)
Conference which took place at the Hague (June–October 1907). This conference, together with the one in 1899, established the concept that the best way to handle international problems was not by war, but through a series of conferences. As a result, the laws of war, peace and neutrality were collected and written down in 14 conventions. Most of the 44 nations who attended signed them, although they were unsuccessful in solving the problems which led to World War I.

Cooperative Societies
Began to be established in the 1820s under the influence of Robert Owen, the owner of a model cotton mill and advocate of trade unions (→ **Owen, Robert**). Some Cooperatives were simply small grocery

stores which tried to cut out shopkeepers' profits by buying goods in bulk and selling them to members at reduced prices. Profits were shared out to customers in proportion to the amount of goods they had bought. The shops were popular because of their low prices and the good quality of their food. In 1863 a Cooperative Wholesale Society (CWS) was established in Manchester. It bought goods from producers in large quantities and supplied individual stores. It soon became a nationwide organization. In 1875 the CWS began manufacturing its own products.

Cotton
The cotton plant can be found in most sub-tropical countries. At the end of the 18th century, Lancashire became the centre of the cotton trade and cotton production in England due to its port Liverpool, its damp and mild climate – ideal for handling cotton thread – and the Pennine streams which provided the energy before the introduction of the steam engine. By the second half of the 19th century, cotton goods were Britain's major export. About nine tenths of these goods were sold abroad, making up nearly one third of Britain's exports. The First World War marked the beginning of the decline of the cotton industry, as the import of raw cotton was greatly affected; moreover, there was an acute shortage of labour, and many export markets were lost. Other countries, such as India, Japan and the USA, began to compete successfully with Britain as they could profit from updated machinery and, in the case of India and Japan, from cheap labour. The decline of the cotton industry and other well-established industries continued after the end of the Second World War. Competition increased, especially from developing countries, and from the spread of man-made fibres such as nylon. In 1979, there were only 66,800 workers left in the British cotton industry out of 710,000 in 1914.

Daily Mail
Morning daily newspaper founded in 1896, published in London. It was widely noted for its foreign coverage of the 1899–1902 war in South Africa and was one of the first British papers to popularize its coverage to appeal to a mass readership.

Darwinism
According to the theory of Charles Darwin (1809–1882), a British biologist, all forms of life evolve or change over a long period of time. Simpler forms of life evolve into more complex forms, and new forms evolve out of older forms. (→ **Social Darwinism**)

Declaratory Act (1766)
Declaration by the British parliament that it had as much right to tax the American colonies and make laws there as in Great Britain. Each new Act added to the colonists' fear of a parliamentary threat to their own established institutions of self-government.

Factory Acts (1833)
These were laws to regulate the conditions of work in British factories. In the course of the Industrial Revolution, the complaints about long working hours and unhealthy conditions caused a campaign for reform led by clergymen, doctors and manufacturers like Sir Robert Peel (senior). The early factory acts were ineffective as no real provision for enforcing the law was made. The first breakthrough came in 1833 with the passing of the Althorp Factory Act, which stated that children between the ages of 9 and 13 were to work a maximum of 9 hours a day and 48 hours a week.

Factory system
The Industrial Revolution eventually took manufacturing out of the home and workshop. Power-driven machines replaced handwork. Poor workers had neither room nor money for these machines in their houses, and factories developed as the best way of bringing together the machines and the workers to operate them. In going to the factories, the workers lost control over working conditions. Their skills were no longer important because the machines now did the work. The Western world began to change from a basically rural and agricultural society to a basically urban and industrial society.

Fashoda Incident (September 1898)
The climax at Fashoda, Egyptian Sudan, of a series of territorial disputes in Africa between Great Britain and France, who were both trying to use the Sudan to link up their different colonial possessions in Africa. Groups of French and British men (under Marchand and Kitchener) set off for Fashoda. The French arrived first, but as both the British and the French wanted to avoid military confrontation, they agreed that Egyptian, British and French flags should fly there together.

Flottenverein (Naval League)
Founded in 1898, in accordance with Tirpitz's politics, to convince the German people of the need for Germany to be a strong sea power and have a powerful navy in case of war.

Flying shuttle
A new type of shuttle invented by John Kay in the 1730s. The cross-thread was no longer thrown by hand, but transported across the loom with the help of two hammers which were moved by cords and a lever. The loom could now weave broader cloth and the weaving process was speeded up. (→ **spinning mule**)

French and Indian War
In 1756 war broke out between Britain and its biggest colonial rival, France. It started in Europe with the Seven Years' War, in which Britain and France supported different sides. This led to war in India and North America, too. In 1760, after a long struggle, Britain (with the help of the American colonists) defeated the French and their allies, the Indians. In 1763, the Peace of Paris was signed: France lost North America, the West Indies and India to England. Britain's Empire had grown much bigger, but its financial situation had become worse because the wars had been very expensive.

Great Exhibition, The (1851)
Planned by Prince Albert, President of the Royal Society of Arts, which suggested the idea of a display of the latest industrial, scientific and artistic achievements from all over the world. It took place in Hyde Park in a revolutionary glass building designed specially for it. The "Crystal Palace" was completed in a record 7 months. The exhibition showed more than 14,000 exhibits – models of bridges, lighthouses, steam locomotives, telescopes, cameras, furniture and china. It was a display of human achievement at its height, ignoring its darker side: poverty, pollution, disease and slums. More than 6 million people visited the exhibition.

Herero
Bantu tribe of cattle breeders in what today is Namibia, South West Africa. When German colonial settlers began to claim their land and change their society, they feared the beginnings of brutal German rule in their country. They rose up against the Germans in a rebellion which lasted from 1904 to 1907. On General von Trotha's orders, almost 80% of the Herero tribe were massacred and many of those who survived were resettled to live on reservations. Trotha wanted the whole tribe to be destroyed, but Wilhelm II and von Bülow modified his orders. All the natives' rights and property were taken from them, they were forced to sign an agreement to work for the German colonists and came completely under their control.

Iron and steel
The cheapest and most useful metals known to man. Iron has been used by man for thousands of years. In the centuries before the Industrial Revolution, all work was done by hand. The ore was heated in a furnace, then hammered out on anvils. Hand-operated bellows were used to keep the fire blazing. Fuel was either wood or coal, so most of the work was done by local workers in rural areas. Ironworkers had not learned how to heat the iron ore enough to melt it. Therefore, they could not control the quality of the iron they made. Ironmaking techniques continued to improve as iron production expanded. In the 1800s the demand for wrought iron to make steam engines, locomotives and railway rails rapidly created a huge iron industry in Europe and the United States. Steel, a mixture of iron and other metals, was made in small quantities at this time, but was still more expensive than iron. In

1856 – an important year in the history of steel – the Bessemer process (named after the British engineer and inventor Henry Bessemer, 1813–98) was successfully introduced into Britain. It was a method of making steel from pig iron and producing it cheaply in large quantities. This easy availability of steel led to many industrial processes being greatly changed. As steel replaced iron as the main building material (e. g. the Eiffel tower), large scale manufacture for constructional purposes began. In Britain, steel production went up from 2 million tonnes in 1880 to 7 million in 1914. In the USA, it rose from 1.5 to 31 million tonnes.

John Bull
Nickname for the English, originally represented in a political satire of 1712 by John Arbuthnot as a kind-hearted farmer, personifying the openness and solidity of the English character.

Kopfsteuer *(hist.: poll tax)*
The most basic form of tax, which does not take a person's income into consideration and is therefore the most unfair form of taxation, since it takes the same amount from the poor as from the rich. Rarely used today, except in a few colonial areas.

Kraal
African village of huts

Lebensraum
Originally a term used in biology to describe the amount of space taken up by a living creature. With growing nationalism in Germany in the 19th century, it was used in a political sense. Also used in Nazi ideology to justify the expansion of the German Empire.

Manchester
Manchester could claim to be the first of the new generation of huge industrial cities created in the Western world during the past 250 years. By 1851 its textile industry (mainly cotton) had developed so much that it had become a major manufacturing and commercial city and Britain's 2nd most important city. Other cities of importance during the Industrial Revolution were: **Liverpool**, which became the second most important port in Britain and grew rapidly as a result of trade with the Americas and the West Indies, as well as the Liverpool-Manchester railway, which opened in 1830 and was the first railway in Britain to link two major cities; **Birmingham**, home of the engineers James Watt and Matthew Boulton, who greatly contributed to the technological progress of the country by developing the steam engine for industrial use there; **Glasgow**, which expanded greatly when trade with the Americas developed in the 18th century and which became the industrial centre of Scotland with its coal, ship-building and engineering industries; and **Blackpool**, famous seaside resort in Lancashire which grew rapidly in the 19th century due to the introduction of fast railway services, its proximity to the Lancashire industrial towns and the writings of William Hutton, a British scientist, who popularized the health-giving properties of seawater.

Manufacturing systems
Before the Industrial Revolution, manufacturing was done by hand or simple machines. Most people worked at home in rural areas. This system of manufacturing was known as the 'domestic system'. The whole family worked together making clothing, food products, textiles, and wood products. The workers themselves provided most of the power for manufacturing. The father was his own master and could therefore control the working conditions for his family. The workers were very skilled. Usually the family worked for one person who bought their goods regularly, and there was little danger of unemployment.

Mercantilism
Economic theory and practice common in Europe from the 16th to the 18th century, according to which the European powers moulded the economies of their colonies to fit their own trading needs and increase their power above that of rival nations. In the 17th and 18th centuries, for example, England passed a series of laws to strengthen its control over the economy of the American colonies. Some of these laws required the American colonists to trade almost entirely with Great Britain or other British colonies, and to use only British ships. Colonies were supposed to serve as export markets and suppliers of raw materials, but manufacturing itself was forbidden in the colonies, so that the colonists had to depend largely on the mother country for manufactured goods. To encourage the Americans to export goods needed by Great Britain, the British granted certain trading privileges for such goods. Other European nations handled trade with their colonies in a similar way.

Mines Act (1842)
Following the passing of the Factory Acts, a Royal Commission on the employment of women and children in mines was appointed. Its report showed the dangerous and hard jobs children had to do. The public was deeply shocked. The Mines Act forbade employment underground of women, girls and boys under the age of ten. Many women were annoyed that they could no longer earn much needed money.

Money values
The standard unit of money in Britain today is the pound, divided into 100 pence. In the 18th and 19th centuries, it was still divided according to a non-decimal system, that is 12 pence (d.) made a shilling (s.), 20 shillings made a pound. This table shows the modern equivalent of money values during the Industrial Revolution:

Old money			new pence
2.4d			1p
6d			2.5p
12d	1s		5p
	10s		50p
240d	20s	£1	100p

Monopoly
The complete dominance of the market by one supplier of a product. The supplier can set prices as high as he/she wishes without fear of competition from others and will make a large profit.

Moroccan Crises (1906, 1911)
Two international crises centering on France's attempts to control Morocco and Germany's attempts to stop France from doing so. The first crisis ended in 1906 at a conference in Spain. German and other national economic rights were upheld, and the French and Spanish were entrusted with keeping order in Morocco. The second crisis began when a German gunboat was sent to Morocco, supposedly to look after German interests, but really to check on the French. It ended with France being given the right to control Morocco, and Germany being given strips of territory from the French Congo in return.

Municipal Corporations Act (1835)
One of the reasons for the lack of public health facilities was the absence of effective local government. The Municipal Corporation Act provided a mayor and councillors to run the affairs of a town. It became compulsory for councils to form a police force. Councils were also responsible for social improvements such as proper drainage and making the streets cleaner.

Navigation Act
A law in Britain passed between 1650 and 1696, designed to increase Britain's role in carrying trade overseas. It stated that all imports to England had to be in English ships or in those of the country of origin. The law remained until 1849 and caused much bad feeling between Britain and the 13 American colonies.

Ned Ludd
Said to have been a Leicestershire workman who broke into a house and destroyed two framework knitting machines in 1779. In 1811 and 1812 there were serious outbreaks of machine-breaking and factory-burning in Lancashire, Yorkshire and Nottinghamshire. The rioters, known as Luddites, were said to have been organized by Ned Ludd.

Norfolk four-course rotation
A farming method, developed in the 17th century, of growing different crops at different times on the same land. Rotating the crops meant that the land was always being used effectively and did not have to be left to lie fallow for a year.

Official blue book
A British parliamentary or other official publication, bound in a blue cover.

Pennsylvania Evening Post
The first daily American newspaper. Began in Philadelphia in 1783.

Pennsylvania Journal
A newspaper established in 1742, dedicated to supporting the American colonists against British rule. When the British imposed their Stamp Tax on the press in 1756, the journal was printed with a skull and crossbones across the top and black borders, signifying the death of freedom of the press.

Pennsylvanischer Staatsbote
Published 1762-1779 by John Heinrich Miller. The most widely read German newspaper in the American colonies (with a circulation of about 6,500). It influenced the German population towards the patriotic cause. Various special supplements were issued, such as the special farewell number which appeared before enforcement of the Stamp Act, Oct. 1765. Although the act taxed all newspapers, it doubled the amount of tax on non-English papers. This paper was the first to announce (on July 9, 1776) the adoption of the *Declaration of Independence*. When the British occupied Philadelphia in 1777, Miller had to flee, but he returned when they left the following year and continued publishing.

Pickelhaube (spiked helmet)
A helmet made from steel or leather with metal parts, with a spike on top. Introduced into the Prussian army in 1842 and worn in the German army in a modified form until World War I.

Pilgrims (AE), **Pilgrim Fathers** (BE)
A group of Puritans (→) who emigrated to North America in 1620 because they were not allowed to practise their religion freely in England. Some of them had been prosecuted because they weren't members of the Church of England. They left from Plymouth on board the *Mayflower*. In early November, the Pilgrims anchored at Cape Cod/Massachusetts. During the first winter in their settlement on the other side of Cape Cod Bay, half of the settlers died. In spring 1621, American Indians found them and showed them how to fish locally and how to plant and grow Indian corn. The first harvest was celebrated by a *Thanksgiving* feast in autumn 1621. It is still an official holiday in the USA today.

Poor Richard's Almanac
Written by Benjamin Franklin (→), one edition per year from 1733 to 1758. It became one of the most popular works printed in colonial America. It included practical advice, jokes, poems, proverbs, e.g. "Early to bed and early to rise, makes a man healthy, wealthy and wise", expressing Franklin's ideas on duty, hard work and simplicity. It had a big influence on American thought before and after the Revolutionary War (1775–1783).

Potato Famine
During the early 1800s, Ireland's population grew rapidly. About half the people lived on small farms that produced little income. Others leased land on estates and had to pay high rents to landlords. Because of their poverty, most of the Irish people depended on potatoes for food. But from 1845 to 1847, Ireland's potato crop failed because of a plant disease. About 750,000 people died of starvation or disease, and hundreds of thousands emigrated, many to the United States.

Power loom
A new loom invented in 1785 by the clergyman Edmund Cartwright. It was driven by a steam engine – the weaver only had to repair broken threads. As a result of the power loom, steam mills became more important and the cotton industry surged ahead of the woollen industry.

Punch
English illustrated periodical which provided weekly comment on British life. Famous for its satiric humour, caricatures and cartoons. Founded in 1841, last issue April 1992.

Puritans
Puritans were English Protestants who wanted to "purify" the Church of England and make it less like the Catholic Church. They wanted church services to be simple and plain and churches to look plainer too, without crosses, candles, pictures and statues. Some Puritans believed they should show their religion by living very simply. They wore simple, dark clothes, worked hard and disapproved of pleasures like dancing and theatre-going. In England, the Puritans weren't allowed to live and practise their religion as they wished, some of them even being sent to prison.

Royal Charter
A document signed by the king, giving special rights and freedoms to a person or an organization, often stating the principles, duties and forms of organization to be observed.

Scramble (the ~ for Africa)
Term describing the race between the Western powers in the 19th century to acquire large areas of Africa and impose colonial rule there.

Social Darwinism
(→ Darwinism) The English philosopher Herbert Spencer (1820–1903) turned Darwin's biological theory into a social theory which stated that all human life is a struggle for existence in which only the fittest survive. The theories of people like Spencer are called "Social Darwinism".

Spinning
Process of making thread from wool, cotton, etc., by drawing it out and twisting it. The shorn fleece of the sheep is "carded", i.e. brushed to make the separate fibres stretch in one direction. The fibres are then twisted together by the movement of a spindle to form a strong thread. The thread is wound up on the spindle. The process was later mechanized.

Spinning jenny/spinning mule
In 1765 James Hargreaves, a Blackburn weaver, turned the traditional spinning-wheel into a new machine: the spinning jenny. By turning a handle, a worker was able to spin several threads and to fill many spindles at once. The spinning mule was invented in 1779 by Samuel Crompton, a cotton spinner. It worked in nearly the same way, but produced stronger yarn of fine quality. It was powered by steam and did the work of about 650 handspinners. His mule of 1792, which worked by itself, could be supervised by a child.

Spirit of '76
Famous patriotic scene painted about 1875 by the American artist Archibald M. Willard (1837–1918). The scene shows a fife player and two drummers leading American troops in a battle in the Revolutionary War (1765–1788).

Splendid isolation
Term used to describe the policy pursued by Britain from 1890 to 1907 of avoiding links with other countries, diplomatically and commercially.

Stamp Act (1765)
A tax placed on all colonial newspapers, legal papers, pamphlets, cards, almanacs, etc. This was the first attempt by the British parliament to make money by taxing the American colonies.

Stars and Stripes
The American flag. It has 13 red and white stripes representing the 13 English colonies which became the first American states, and 50 white stars representing the number of states today.

Statue of Liberty
Statue presented by the French to the Americans in 1886, as a gift. It stands at the entrance to New York harbour and greets immigrants from all over the world, the torch symbolizing the light of freedom and a new life. Its formal title is "Liberty Enlightening the World". Inscribed on the statue's left arm is the date of the signing of the Declaration of Independence.

Suez Canal
100-mile-long shipping canal built 1859–1869, designed by the French engineer Ferdinand de Lesseps. Provides the shortest route for international sea traffic between Europe and Asia. The project was made possible by means of European loans and investments. In return, Egypt's ruler promised the free passage of European ships. When, in 1875, the Egyptian ruler sold the canal shares to avoid bankruptcy, Disraeli, the British Prime Minister, bought majority shares in it for £4 million and it came under British control. It provided an important link in the British Empire for over 75 years.

Sugar Act (1764)
British law which placed heavy taxes on sugar imported into the colonies from the French and Dutch West Indies, giving a monopoly to British West Indies sugar planters.

Times, The (founded 1785)
Daily newspaper published in London. One of Britain's oldest and most influential newspapers. By the mid 1800s, it had become a widely respected influence on British public opinion. Originally often critical of government policy, it came to be ruled by tradition, although its editorial views were independent, articulate and strong.

Townshend Duties (1767)
Taxes the British parliament placed on 5 types of goods imported into the American colonies after the failure of the Stamp Act. In 1770, after many objections, 4 of the categories were removed. The 5th one, on tea, stayed until the *Boston Tea Party*. Named after the British Chancellor of the Exchequer, Charles Townshend.

Transvaal
Most northerly province of the Republic of South Africa. The most important industrial area of southern Africa, producing the most gold in the world. Main towns include Johannesburg, Krugersdorp and Vereeniging. From 1835 onwards, many white Africans (Boers) who were unhappy with British rule in the Cape Colony fled to the Transvaal. Established as an independent republic in 1852. It was annexed by the British in 1877, which led to rebellion and the Boer War of 1880–1881. Following the Boers' victory, the British recognized the independence of the Transvaal. It was annexed in 1900 as a British colony, but allowed self-government in 1906. It joined the Union of South Africa in 1910.

Tribute work
Colonial economic policy. Nations increased their wealth by forcing conquered peoples to work for them and to make payments called *tribute* in return for protection.

Uncle Sam
Personification of the nation or people of the UNited States of AMerica. The name arose from the frequent appearance of the initials US on government supplies for the army in the war of 1812. The stripes on the hat and the trousers and the stars on the hat represent the thirteen original states.

Union Jack
Flag of the United Kingdom, combining the crosses of St. George (England), St. Andrew (Scotland), and St. Patrick (Ireland). The earliest form of the flag developed in 1606 with the "union" of England and Scotland. "Jack" comes from "jack staff" – a small flagstaff on a ship where a flag is flown to show the ship's nationality.

Weaving
Method of making fabric. Vertical threads are stretched out on a loom; a shuttle transports a horizontal thread back and forth, passing over and under the vertical threads and producing a strip of cloth.

Workhouse
In Britain, formerly a place where very poor people who had no employment or were too old to work were sent to live and work. After the Poor Law Amendment Act (1834), there was a policy to build more workhouses and place as many paupers as possible in them, but living conditions were very bad and people were afraid of having to go there. They were much criticized by reformers, who revealed many "workhouse scandals".

Biographies

Biko, Stephen (1946–1977)
Born Kingwilliamstown, Cape Province (South Africa). Became involved in political activity during his student days. First president of the SASO (South African Students' Organization). Worked for BCP (Black Community Programmes) in Durban but was banned in 1973, along with seven other SASO leaders. Restricted to his home, he worked as Branch Executive of the Eastern Cape Branch of BCP until he too was banned from working for the BCP. Was charged many times under security legislation, but never convicted. Appointed Honorary President of the BPC (Black People's Convention), an organization he helped to found. In 1977 he was imprisoned under the Terrorism Act. He was kept naked and chained and died less than a month later, after being tortured. The cause of death was later established as brain damage.

Boulton, Matthew (1728–1809)
A Birmingham metalwork manufacturer. His works at Soho near Birmingham were opened in 1762. They were powered by a waterwheel. Boulton was concerned by summer water shortages and was looking for a way to solve this problem. He met James Watt in 1768. In 1773 they went into partnership. Boulton provided the necessary capital and his factory contained the skilled workers Watt needed to build his steam engine. Only after several years of constant money worries could they enjoy the profits of their joint venture.

Bülow, Prince Bernhard von
(1849–1929) 1897–1900: German Foreign Secretary, 1900–1909: German Chancellor. In foreign affairs Bülow was notably influenced by the ambitious naval plans of Admiral von Tirpitz and supported the Emperor's wish for Germany's political and geographical expansion.

Chamberlain, Joseph (1836–1914)
Politician, social reformer and architect of the imperialist policies carried out by the British government at the beginning of the 20th century. 1895–1903: Secretary of State for the colonies. He was strongly involved in South African affairs and supported British rule over the Boer republic of Transvaal. His imperialism was widely accepted by the industrial masses with their increasing nationalism. He announced a new system of taxes favourable to Britain, which he hoped would draw Britain and its colonies together in a kind of common market. He wanted to strengthen Britain's international security and protect her

manufacturers, who were threatened by new competition from the United States and Germany. This protectionism was against the principle of free trade, which meant cheap bread for the masses. Because of this, the Liberal Unionists were defeated in the general elections of 1906.

Disraeli, Benjamin (1800–1881)
Conservative Member of Parliament; British Prime Minister in 1868 and 1874–1880. He worked on a programme of social reforms which won him the support of the masses. By a series of factory acts, he prevented the exploitation of the labour force and by trade union acts, he strengthened the legal position of these organizations. More important than his domestic programme, however, was his imperial and foreign policy. He furthered Great Britain's colonial aims in Africa and India and was keen to make the country more respected and powerful abroad. He bought the Suez canal shares from the ruler of Egypt. In 1876 he succeeded in giving Queen Victoria the title Empress of India. His skilful diplomacy at the Congress of Berlin (1878) helped to keep the peace in Europe after conflict between the Russians and the Turks in the Balkans had caused British concern over the safety of the route to India.

Fisher, John Arbuthnot (1841–1920)
British admiral and first sea lord. He reformed the Royal Navy during World War I and was responsible for the construction of the battleship *Dreadnought*, which was immediately copied by Germany. It established the pattern of the warship that dominated the world's navies for almost 40 years. Another creation was the lightly armoured *Invincible* battle cruiser. This type carried heavy armament but relied on speed for its protection.

Franklin, Benjamin (1706–1790)
Born in Boston, Massachusetts. Became famous as a diplomat, politician, writer and publisher. He wrote *Poor Richard's Almanach*, and was editor of the *Pennsylvania Gazette*. President of the state of Pennsylvania three times. 1757–1775: represented Pennsylvania in London. He defended the rights of the American colonies in Parliament and criticized the British government's tax policy towards the colonies. In 1775 he was involved in writing the Declaration of Independence and was also successful in getting Britain to recognize US independence. From 1776–1785 Franklin served as American ambassador in France where he was very popular. He persuaded France to support the American rebels in the American Revolution.

George III (1760–1820)
British King. Victim of an inherited disease which sometimes made him seem quite mad. He wanted to make himself absolute ruler of the country and its colonies, but only succeeded in strengthening the power of the parliament. He and his Chief Minister, Lord North, lost the American colonies during the American Revolution.

Gladstone, William Ewart (1809–1898)
British statesman. Prime Minister: 1868–74, 1880–85, 1886, 1892–94. As a strict Anglican, he tried to apply his Christian principles to politics, especially in domestic and foreign affairs. Under his leadership many social and political reforms were carried out.

Hardie, James Keir (1856–1915)
Born in Scotland in a one-roomed house, the eldest of 9 children. By the age of 10 he had started working in a coal-mine. In 1892 he stood for parliament and became the first independent Labour Member of Parliament. He did more than anyone to create the modern Labour Party and is still one of its heroes.

Hudson, George (1800–1871)
An English financier who began his career as an apprentice in the drapery business. In 1827 he started his railway activities by investing £30,000, which he had inherited, in railway shares. He was also politically active – three times Mayor of York and Member of Parliament in 1845. By 1848 he had control of a third of all railways in Britain. In 1849 many of his companies went bankrupt and he was taken to court. It turned out that many of his railway-building schemes had been dishonest. Hudson was forced to resign and fled to Paris owing shareholders thousands of pounds.

Ismail Pasha (1830–1895)
Became viceroy of Egypt in 1863, under the supremacy of the Sultan. He began many reforms in education and jurisdiction as well as in the infrastructure of the country, building canals, bridges, railways and factories. This, along with the building of the Suez Canal, increased Egypt's debts enormously and to avoid bankruptcy, he sold the canal shares to the British government.

Jefferson, Thomas (1743–1826)
President of the USA from 1801–1809. Born in Virginia, studied law and became a delegate of the Continental Congress. In 1776 he and Benjamin Franklin wrote the Declaration of Independence. 1785–1789: Minister to France. 1789–1793: first Secretary of State of the USA.

Jenner, Edward (1744–1823)
English surgeon and discoverer of vaccination for smallpox. Before the introduction of the first satisfactory method of preventing the disease, about one in ten people who caught it died. The only means of fighting the disease was the so-called innoculation, an injection of a mild form of the disease in the hope of making the patient immune to further infection.

Jühlke, Karl Ludwig (1856–1886)
German politician and supporter of German colonialism; good friend of Carl Peters, whom he accompanied on his African journeys. Murdered on the coast of Somalia.

Kitchener, (Horatio) Herbert (1850–1916) British field marshal, statesman and imperial administrator. Secretary for War at the beginning of World War I. As commander of the Egyptian army, he won back the Sudan for Egypt at the battle of Omdurman in 1898. In the same year, he tactfully and successfully handled the Fashoda crisis by preventing French sovereignty over the Sudan. As commander-in-chief in the South African War of 1899–1902, he broke Boer resistance by methods such as burning Boer farms and driving Boer women and children into concentration camps, thereby ending the war.

Kruger, Paul (1825–1904)
Farmer, soldier and statesman of Dutch descent. In South African history, he is regarded as the builder of the so-called Afrikaner (Boer) nation. During the period of British imperialism in Africa, he fought for the independence of the Transvaal, the South African Republic. He won several military victories against the British. In 1881 he negotiated a peace which gave the republic a limited independence. President from 1883 to 1902. In the 1899–1902 Boer War, his troops finally had to accept British supremacy, and he was sent to Holland.

Lesseps, Ferdinand, Vicomte de (1805–1894) French engineer and diplomat. During his diplomatic service in Alexandria, Egypt, he took up an old idea of connecting the Red and the Mediterranean Seas by way of a canal. With the official approval of the Egyptian ruler, work on the Suez Canal began in 1859.

Lister, Joseph (1827–1912)
A surgeon at the Glasgow Royal Infirmary. Lister noted that patients often survived an operation but then died of infection of the wound. He realized the importance of cleanliness. When he read about the discoveries of Louis Pasteur, a French scientist who had shown that bacteria were present in the atmosphere, he decided to apply Pasteur's theories to the infections of wounds and to clean the wound and disinfect hands, instruments and the operating theatre. His methods were sucessful but he was attacked by his colleagues who accused him of having a 'mania for cleanliness'.

Lovett, William (1800–1877)
A cabinet maker by trade. In 1836 he and a group of skilled tradesmen and small shopkeepers set up the London Working Men's Association which aimed "to seek by every legal means to place all the classes of

society in possession of equal political and social rights". In 1838 they drew up a charter of their demands, the People's Charter, but it was finally rejected by Parliament. Lovett left the Chartist movement and worked for the education and schooling of the working people. In 1843 he established a Sunday school which became the centre for his educational ideas based on Cooperative principles (→ **Cooperative societies**).

Lugard, Frederick (1858–1945)
British soldier and colonial administrator. As governor-general, Lugard administered Nigeria from 1912 to 1919, Britain's largest African colony. His practice of indirect rule tolerated traditional chiefdoms, native institutions and customs. His administrative concept came to serve as a model for the rule of other African British colonies.

Mandela, Nelson (1918–   )
Worked hard towards ending the policy of apartheid in South Africa. He established the military wing of the African National Congress. In 1964 he was imprisoned for life for his work in trying to overthrow the S. African government and assisting an armed invasion of S. Africa. He was released in 1990 and went back to a peaceful, political struggle. As a result of engaging all political parties in talks with the "white" government, he was instrumental in bringing about the end of apartheid. He became president of the ANC and was awarded the Nobel Peace Prize in 1993. In 1994 the ANC won the majority of seats in the first free general elections in S. Africa and Mandela was made president.

Marchand, Jean Baptiste (1863–1934)
French soldier and explorer. Became famous for his occupation of Fashoda (now Kodok), Sudan. Caused a Franco-British crisis by hoisting the French flag at Fashoda in 1898. Afterwards became the idol of the French nation because of his bravery in crossing Africa and confronting British colonial policy in the Sudan.

Owen, Robert (1771–1858)
British social reformer. In 1800 he became manager of the New Lanark cotton mills, Lanarkshire, where he set up a social welfare programme and established a "model community". His socialist theories were put to the test in other experimental communities, but all were unsuccessful. He was later active in the trade-union movement.

Pearson, Karl (1857–1936)
British mathematician and one of the founders of modern statistics. He helped to create the science of biometry (the statistical aspects of biology). He became involved in applying statistics to biological problems of heredity and evolution. He believed that environment had little to do with the development of mental or emotional qualities. He felt that the high birth rate of the poor was a threat to civilization and that the "higher" races should replace the "lower".

Peel, Robert, Jr. (1788–1850)
British Prime Minister 1834–1835 and 1841–1846. Thanks to his father's influence, he became a Member of Parliament at the age of 21, supporting the Tory (Conservative) Party. He also founded the first police force and policemen were called 'Bobbies' and 'Peelers' after him. To help the poor, Peel reduced the taxes on goods, especially food, and brought back income tax instead. He was later thought of as the founder of modern conservatism.

Peel, Robert, Sr. (1750–1830)
Wealthy cotton manufacturer and calico printer. Member of Parliament from 1790, made a baronet in 1800. His money secured his son his first parliamentary seat.

Peters, Carl (1856–1918)
German explorer; studied British principles of colonisation. In 1884 he founded the Society for German Colonization (Gesellschaft für Deutsche Kolonisation). By a number of contracts with tribal chiefs who gave their territories to him, he established the German East Africa protectorate of Tanganyika (today part of Tanzania). He tried to expand German influence by establishing the German East Africa Company. Without German governmental support, he agreed on a treaty with the King of Uganda in 1890. This treaty was declared invalid by the German government, which had accepted that Uganda belonged to a sphere of British influence.

Rhodes, Cecil (1853–1902)
Began his career as a financier and gained control of South Africa's mining industry (diamonds and gold). Became a member of the Cape Colony parliament in 1881 and Prime Minister of the Cape Colony in 1890. In 1895 he was involved in the *Jameson Raid*, an attempt to overthrow the Boer-dominated government of Paul Kruger, and was forced to resign in 1896. His aim was to make the whole of Africa British. He expanded British territory northward to Mashonaland and Matabeleland (named Rhodesia in his honour, today Zambia). Wherever he travelled, he promoted his plans for spanning Africa by railway and telegraph.

Salisbury, Robert Cecil, 3rd marquess of, (1830–1903)
British Conservative political leader. Accompanied Disraeli to the Berlin Conference in 1878. Prime Minister in 1885, 1886–1892 and 1895–1902. Took a great interest in foreign and imperial affairs. Salisbury believed that European rule, preferably British, was necessary for the advancement of the "backward" races. During his time as prime minister, there were serious conflicts and rivalries between Britain and the great European powers and it was largely thanks to his patience and diplomacy that war was avoided. He remained at the head of the government during the 1889–1902 Boer War, retiring from public life in 1902.

Stephenson, George (1781–1848)
Began his career as an assistant colliery fireman. His employer noticed his engineering skills and provided him with money to build a locomotive. On its first run in 1814, Stephenson's first locomotive, *Blücher* (named after a Prussian general), travelled at seven kilometres per hour, pulling thirty tons of coal in eight loaded wagons. Over the following years, Stephenson gained a good reputation as an engineer of locomotives. A wealthy landowner, Edward Pease, who planned a railway line for transporting coal from Darlington to Stockton, invited Stephenson to be the engineer for the line. On 27 September 1825, the opening ceremony of the Stockton-Darlington railway line was witnessed by 50,000 people. The line proved to be profitable to the coal-mining industry. Industrialists in Liverpool and Manchester were dissatisfied with the monopoly of the Bridgewater Canal Company in transporting their goods and in 1824 they engaged Stephenson as the chief engineer for a 40 mile (64 km) railway line between the two cities. Stephenson faced a lot of opposition, especially by the Bridgewater Canal Company, which spread propaganda about the dangers that locomotives would bring, such as pollution, terrifying livestock, and blinding and deafening passengers. But in 1826 the Liverpool-Manchester railway was finally authorized by Parliament. The company offered a £500 prize for the best steam engine on the new line. Stephenson's locomotive *The Rocket* won with a top speed of 27 miles (43 kilometres) per hour. In 1830 the two-way track between Liverpool and Manchester was opened. Goods delivered in Manchester were received in Liverpool the same day, by canal it took three days.

Tirpitz, Alfred (1849–1930)
Admiral and politician. As Secretary of State of the Imperial Navy Department, he had a strong influence on German foreign policy before World War I. He was the builder of the German high seas fleet, built to rival the British Royal Navy.

Tull, Jethro (1674–1741)
An English agronomist and inventor. Tull was dissatisfied with the traditional method of sowing. He invented a horse-drawn seed drill which could sow seeds in straight rows at the same depth. He claimed he could double his crops using only a third of the previous quantity of seed. Tull's ideas helped to form the basis of modern British agriculture.

Queen Victoria (1819–1901, reigned 1837–1901)
Queen Victoria came to the throne at the age of 18. Three years later she married Albert, a German prince. A sensitive and well-educated man, Albert had more influence on Victoria than anyone else in her life. They had nine children and their family life set an example to the nation. Prince Albert was a great supporter of industrial progress. In 1861 he died from typhoid fever (which he caught from bad drinking water in a royal palace) and left Victoria a mourning widow for the remaining 40 years of her reign. She had little influence on the government of the country which was by now in the hands of Parliament and her two famous Prime Ministers, Gladstone and Disraeli. Yet she became the symbol of the growing British Empire (she was proclaimed Empress of India in 1876), of the expanding economy and of the stability of the British way of life. When she died in 1901 the whole country went into mourning. It was the end of a great era, the Victorian Age.

Washington, George (1732–1799)
Born in Virginia, first President of the USA. He did military service against the French (1755–1759) and was chosen to command the Continental Army against the British in 1775. He presided over the Federal Convention, which adopted the Constitution. He was unanimously elected President of the USA in 1789, retiring in 1797.

Watt, James (1736–1819)
The motive power of steam was no new discovery: Thomas Newcomen had already tried to build a steam engine in 1712. In his spare time, Watt tried to improve a model of the Newcomen machine, but he did not have any money and needed a financial backer. Matthew Boulton (→), the owner of the Soho Hardware works in Birmingham, heard of his problem and told Watt he would provide him with money. In 1774 Watt moved to Birmingham and started work. Eventually, in 1781, Watt invented his sun-and-planet gear. This turned the up-and-down motion of the piston into rotation. The "double action" of the rotary motion steam engine (the piston could now push and pull with equal power, producing two revolutions for each cycle of the engine) was an amazing breakthrough. The engine could be used to drive many different machines and was not just limited to draining mines. Boulton took a big risk by borrowing £17,000 from the bank to put the new engine into production. His boldness paid off. By 1800 there were over 500 Boulton and Watt engines at work in different factories across the country. The engines were used in places such as textile mills, breweries, iron foundries and flour mills. Watt's engines needed accurately made parts in order to work properly. This led to the growth of the machine-tool industry. Later, similar steam engines were used to power railway locomotives and steamships.

Wellington, Duke of (1769–1852)
One of England's greatest generals. Also held many positions in government, including Prime Minister (1828–1830). From 1808 to 1812 he fought successfully against the Napoleonic troops in Portugal and Spain. He was Napoleon's great rival and, together with Prussian forces, defeated him at the Battle of Waterloo in 1815. This marked the end of the Napoleonic Wars and of French dominance in Europe.

Wilhelm I (1797–1888)
Seventh King of Prussia (1861–1888). Formed a friendship with Queen Victoria and Albert. Soon made clear his intention of strengthening the throne and the army. In 1862 he made Bismarck Minister-President of Prussia. Accepted Bismarck's advice on Prussia's political course in Europe for more than two decades. Following the defeat of France and Napoleon III in the Franco-Prussian War, he was proclaimed first German Emperor (1871–1888).

Wilhelm II (1859–1941)
Ninth King of Prussia and third German Emperor (1888–1918). Great admirer of the traditional Prussian ideal of warrior-king. His speeches had German imperialism as their constant theme. In 1896 he sent a telegram to President Kruger of South Africa, congratulating him on the suppression of the *Jameson raid* – an unauthorized raid into the Transvaal in 1895 by Sir Leander Jameson, an administrator in the British South Africa Company. He adopted an anti-British attitude at the start of the Boer War, but was seriously concerned with Anglo-German reconciliation for a while following several visits to England. Despite this, he backed von Tirpitz's plans for a large German navy to match the British navy.

Vocabulary

A

(to) abandon [əˈbændən]	aufgeben, verlassen
(to) abolish [əˈbɒlɪʃ]	abschaffen, aufheben
about	ungefähr
(to) abridge sth.	etw. kürzen
(to) absorb [əbˈsɔːb]	aufnehmen, verschmelzen
accord [əˈkɔːd]	Übereinkunft
of one's own ~	aus eigenem Antrieb, von selbst
of its own ~	von selbst
according to	
~ ~ how …	je nachdem wie …
~ ~ him/her	seiner/ihrer Meinung nach
(to) accumulate [əˈkjuːmjuleɪt]	(sich an-)sammeln
acquisition [ˌækwɪˈzɪʃn]	Erwerb
act (of parliament)	(Parlaments-)Akte; Gesetz
action	Handeln, Aktion
legal ~	legale Aktion
illegal ~	illegale Aktion
(to) add up	zusammenzählen
(to) ~~ to	ergeben, sich belaufen auf
administration	Verwaltung, Regierung
(to) advance [ədˈvɑːns]	vorrücken, vorankommen
affection	Zuneigung
affluent [ˈæfluənt]	reich
afraid [əˈfreɪd]	ängstlich
(to) be afraid (of)	Angst haben (vor)
aghast [əˈɡɑːst]	erschüttert, erschrocken
agrarian	Agrar-, agrarisch
(to) agree	zustimmen
(to) ~ on sth.	einer Sache zustimmen
(to) ~ with sb.	mit jm. einverstanden sein
agriculture [ˈæɡrɪkʌltʃə]	Landwirtschaft
(to) aid [eɪd]	helfen
aim [eɪm]	Ziel
allegiance (to) [əˈliːdʒəns]	Loyalität (gegenüber)
allegorical [ˌælɪˈɡɒrɪkl]	allegorisch
allegory [ˈælɪɡəri]	Allegorie, Sinnbild
(to) allow	ermöglichen, erlauben
almanac [ˈɔːlmənæk]	Almanach
(to) alter [ˈɔːltə]	(ver-)ändern
ambitious [æmˈbɪʃəs]	ehrgeizig
amendment	(Gesetzes-)Änderung, Abänderungsantrag
amount (of) [əˈmaʊnt]	Menge
(to) amount to	sich belaufen auf
anaesthesia [ˌænɪsˈθiːziə]	Anästhesie, Schmerz-/Betäubungsmittel
ancestor [ˈænsestə]	Vorfahre/Vorfahrin
antique [ænˈtiːk]	antik
annual [ˈænjʊəl]	jährlich
antiseptic	antiseptisch, keimtötend
anvil [ˈænvɪl]	Amboß
(to) appear	scheinen
(to) appoint sb. [əˈpɔɪnt]	jn. ernennen, jn. bestimmen
apprentice [əˈprentɪs]	Lehrling, Auszubildende/r
apprenticeship	Lehre, Ausbildung
approval [əˈpruːvl]	Zustimmung, Einwilligung
approximately [əˈprɒksɪmətli]	ungefähr, fast
arbitration [ˌɑːbɪˈtreɪʃn]	Vermittlung, Schlichtung
(to) go to ~	sich einem Schiedsspruch unterwerfen
architecture [ˈɑːkɪtektʃə]	Architektur
area [ˈeəriə]	Gegend, Gebiet
arm [ɑːm]	Waffe
in ~s	bewaffnet
(to) be armed	bewaffnet sein
army	Armee
around	ungefähr
arrogant [ˈærəɡənt]	arrogant, hochnäsig, anmaßend
askari	Askari (hist.: afrikanischer Soldat in Deutsch-Ostafrika)
assassination [əˌsæsɪˈneɪʃn]	Mord
(to) assemble	sich versammeln; zusammenrufen
(to) assume [əˈsjuːm]	ausgehen von, annehmen
at the same time	gleichzeitig
attack	Angriff, Überfall
(to) attack [əˈtæk]	angreifen
authorities (pl.) [ɔːˈθɒrətɪz]	Behörden
(to) authorize [ˈɔːθəraɪz]	ermächtigen
available [əˈveɪləbl]	verfügbar, erhältlich
(to) average [ˈævərɪdʒ]	durchschnittlich betragen

B

back and forth	hin und her
bairn [beən]	(schott., lit.) Baby
balance of trade [ˌbæləns_əf ˈtreɪd]	Handelsbilanz
ballad [ˈbæləd]	Ballade, Lied
ballot [ˈbælət]	Abstimmung
secret ~	geheime Wahl
barbarism [ˈbɑːbərɪzəm]	Barbarei, Grausamkeit
barefoot [ˈbeəfʊt]	barfüßig
barley [ˈbɑːli]	Gerste
basket [ˈbɑːskɪt]	Korb
battle	Schlacht
battleship	Schlachtschiff
bearer [ˈbeərə]	Inhaber/in
(to) beg	betteln
(to) behead [bɪˈhed]	köpfen, enthaupten
bellows [ˈbeləʊz]	Blasebalg
belongings [bɪˈlɒŋɪŋz]	Habe, Eigentum
berlin	(eine Art) Kutsche
(to) betray [bɪˈtreɪ]	verraten, mißbrauchen
bible [ˈbaɪbl]	Bibel
birth certificate [ˈbɜːθ səˌtɪfɪkət]	Geburtsurkunde
blast [blɑːst]	Windstoß, Druckwelle
bloodyback	(hist.) Schimpfwort für britische Soldaten in amerikanischen Kolonien
blossom [ˈblɒsəm]	Blüte
boldness	Kühnheit, Mut
border	Grenze
boundary [ˈbaʊndri]	Grenze, Abgrenzung
(to) bow [baʊ]	verbeugen
(to) box in	(in einem Gehäuse) unterbringen
boycott [ˈbɔɪkɒt]	Boykott
(to) break out	ausbrechen; beginnen
breakwater	Wellenbrecher
breeding	(Auf-)Zucht; Brutstätte
livestock ~ [ˈlaɪvstɒk]	Viehzucht
(to) bring about	verursachen, herbeiführen
bud	Knospe
bulky [ˈbʌlki]	sperrig
(to) bully [ˈbʊli]	einschüchtern
burnous(e) [bɜːˈnuːs]	Burnus

C

c. = circa ['sɜːkə]	zirka
cabinet ['kæbɪnət]	Kabinett
calamity [kə'læməti]	Unheil, Unglück
calico ['kælɪkəʊ]	Kattun
cannon	Kanone
canopy ['kænəpi]	Überdachung
capital	Hauptstadt
cap of liberty ['lɪbəti]	Jakobinermütze
capstan ['kæpstən]	Drehkreuz, Presse; Winde
caring ['keərɪŋ]	fürsorglich
cart	Wagen, Karren
cartoon	Karikatur
cash-crop ['kæʃkrɒp]	zum Verkauf bestimmtes Agrarerzeugnis
(to) catch up with sb./sth.	jn./etw. einholen
cause [kɔːz]	Ursache
~ and effect relationship	Ursache-Wirkung
(to) cause sth.	etw. verursachen
cautious ['kɔːʃəs]	vorsichtig
century	Jahrhundert
cereal ['sɪərɪəl]	Getreide
challenge ['tʃælɪndʒ]	Herausforderung
chandelier [ˌʃændə'lɪə]	Kronleuchter
charcoal ['tʃɑːkəʊl]	Holzkohle
chart	Diagramm, Tabelle
bar ~	Säulendiagramm
flow ~	Flußdiagramm
charter ['tʃɑːtə]	Charta
cheap [tʃiːp]	billig
Chief Justice [ˌtʃiːf 'dʒʌstɪs]	Oberrichter/in, oberste/r Richter/in
chiefdom ['tʃiːfdəm]	Herrschaft
china ['tʃaɪnə]	Porzellan
chronological [ˌkrɒnə'lɒdʒɪkl]	chronologisch
church	Kirche
circumstances ['sɜːkəmstənsɪz]	Umstände
claim [kleɪm]	Anspruch
(to) claim	beanspruchen
(to) clap on [klæp]	halten, fest drücken an
clergyman ['klɜːdʒɪmən]	Geistlicher
climate ['klaɪmɪt]	Klima
clog	Holzschuh
cloth [klɒθ]	Stoff, Tuch
clothing ['kləʊðɪŋ]	Kleidung
clove [kləʊv]	Gewürznelke
clover ['kləʊvə]	Klee
coal	Kohle
coalmine	Bergwerk, Mine
coarse cloth [kɔːs]	(Segel-)Tuch
cogwheel	Zahnrad
coke [kəʊk]	Koks
colliery ['kɒljəri]	Kohlengrube
colonial [kə'ləʊnɪəl]	kolonial
~ power	Kolonialmacht
colonist ['kɒlənɪst]	Kolonist/in; Aussiedler/in
colony ['kɒləni]	Kolonie
column ['kɒləm]	Spalte, Kolumne
comforts ['kʌmfəts]	Luxusgüter
commerce ['kɒmɜːs]	Handel(sverkehr)
commissioner [kə'mɪʃənə]	Beauftragte/r, Kommissar/in
common land	Gemeindeland
commonwealth ['kɒmənwelθ]	Staat, Gemeinwesen
(to) compete with [kəm'piːt]	konkurrieren mit
competition [ˌkɒmpə'tɪʃn]	Wettbewerb, Konkurrenz
(to) conceal from [kən'siːl]	verbergen vor
(to) condense [kən'dens]	komprimieren, kondensieren
(to) conduct [kən'dʌkt]	leiten, anführen
confederation [kənˌfedə'reɪʃn]	Konföderation, (Staaten-)Bund
confined [kən'faɪnd]	begrenzt
conflict ['kɒnflɪkt]	Konflikt, Streit
(to) confound [kən'faʊnd]	verwirren
congress (pol.) ['kɒŋgres]	Kongreß
(to) connect with [kə'nekt]	verbinden mit
~ed with [kə'nektɪd]	zusammenhängend mit, verwandt mit
connecting-rod	Pleuelstange
conscience ['kɒnʃəns]	Gewissen
consent [kən'sent]	Zustimmung, Erlaubnis
(to) consent (to)	zustimmen (zu), einwilligen (in)
consequence ['kɒnsɪkwəns]	Konsequenz, Folge
conservative [kən'sɜːvətɪv]	konservativ
constituency [kən'stɪtjuənsi]	Wahlkreis
(to) constitute ['kɒnstɪtjuːt]	bilden, gründen
constitution [ˌkɒnstɪ'tjuːʃn]	Verfassung
consumption [kən'sʌmpʃn]	Verbrauch, Verzehr
contract ['kɒntrækt]	Vertrag
(to) sign a ~	einen Vertrag unterzeichnen
contrast ['kɒntrɑːst]	Gegensatz
(to) contrast [kən'trɑːst]	kontrastieren, im Gegensatz stehen
(to) control [kən'trəʊl]	kontrollieren
convenience [kən'viːnɪəns]	Toilette
cooperation [kəʊˌɒpə'reɪʃn]	Mitarbeit, Zusammenarbeit
copper	Kupfer
copra ['kɒprə]	Kopra
corded	mit Stricken versehen
corruption [kə'rʌpʃn]	Korruption
cosy ['kəʊzi]	gemütlich, bequem
cottage ['kɒtɪdʒ]	Häuschen
cotton ['kɒtn]	Baumwolle
~ mill	Baumwollspinnerei
councillor ['kaʊnsələ]	Stadtrat/Stadträtin
coup d'état [ˌkuː deɪ'tɑː]	Staatsstreich
cow	Kuh
(to) crawl [krɔːl]	kriechen
(to) create [kri'eɪt]	schaffen, erfinden
crisis ['kraɪsɪs]	Krise
crocodile ['krɒkədaɪl]	Krokodil
crop	Feldfrucht
~ rotation	Fruchtfolge
crow [krəʊ]	Krähe
(to) cruise [kruːz]	kreuzen (mit dem Schiff)
crystal ['krɪstl]	Kristall
(to) curb sb.'s influence [kɜːb]	jemandes Einfluß einschränken
curious ['kjʊərɪəs]	neugierig
current ['kʌrənt]	Strömung
(to) be cut off from	abgeschnitten sein von
cwt ≈ hundredweight	Zentner
cylinder ['sɪlɪndə]	Zylinder
lower ~	unterer Zylinder
upper ~	oberer Zylinder

D

damp	feucht
dangerous	gefährlich
(to) dare	wagen, sich trauen
data (pl.) ['deɪtə]	Angaben
deal	Geschäft
(to) make/do a ~ with	ein Geschäft abschließen mit
debtor's prison ['detə]	(hist.) Schuldnergefängnis
debts (pl.) [dets]	Schulden
Declaration of the Rights of Man	Erklärung der Menschen- und Bürgerrechte

(to) **decorate** ['dekəreɪt]	schmücken
decoration	Schmuck, Verzierung
decrease ['diːkriːs]	Abnahme, Rückgang
(to) **decrease** [ˌdiːˈkriːs]	abnehmen, nachlassen
(to) **defeat** [dɪˈfiːt]	besiegen
(to) **defend** [dɪˈfend]	verteidigen
(to) **defy** [dɪˈfaɪ]	sich widersetzen
delay [dɪˈleɪ]	Verzögerung
without ~	unverzüglich
delegate ['delɪgət]	Vertreter/in
(to) **deliver** [dɪˈlɪvə]	aushändigen, übergeben; entbinden, gebären
demand	Nachfrage; Forderung
(to) **demand** [dɪˈmɑːnd]	fordern
demonstration [ˌdemənˈstreɪʃn]	Demonstration
(to) **depend on** [dɪˈpend]	abhängen von
(to) **derive** [dɪˈraɪv]	ableiten, herleiten
desecration [ˌdesɪˈkreɪʃn]	Entweihung, Schändung
(to) **desert** [dɪˈzɜːt]	verlassen, im Stich lassen
(to) **desire** [dɪˈzaɪə]	sich wünschen, sich sehnen nach
destination [ˌdestɪˈneɪʃn]	Ziel(ort)
determined [dɪˈtɜːmɪnd]	(fest) entschlossen, bestimmt
(to) **die out**	aussterben
(to) **dig**	graben
(to) **disagree**	nicht übereinstimmen; nicht einer Meinung sein
disarmament [dɪsˈɑːməmənt]	Abrüstung
disaster [dɪˈzɑːstə]	Katastrophe, Unglück
disgrace [dɪsˈgreɪs]	Schande, Ungnade
(to) **dislike**	nicht mögen
dismal ['dɪzməl]	trist, düster, bedrückend
(to) **dismiss** sb. [dɪsˈmɪs]	jn. entlassen
display [dɪˈspleɪ]	(Ausstellungs-)Stand
(to) **dissolve** [dɪˈzɒlv]	auflösen
distribution [ˌdɪstrɪˈbjuːʃn]	Verteilung
diversity [daɪˈvɜːsəti]	Vielfalt
(to) **divide up**	aufteilen
doleful	traurig
dolorous ['dɒlərəs]	düster, trist, schwermütig
dominion [dəˈmɪniən]	Herrschaft(sgebiet)
(to) **double** ['dʌbl]	verdoppeln
(to) **doubt** [daʊt]	zweifeln an
doubtful	zweifelhaft
(to) **drag**	ziehen, schleppen
drain	Abfluß
(to) **drain**	trockenlegen, entwässern
drainage ['dreɪnɪdʒ]	Entwässerung
dreadful ['dredfl]	schrecklich, furchtbar
(to) **drive** sb. **out**	jn. vertreiben
duration [djuˈreɪʃn]	Dauer
dusty ['dʌsti]	verstaubt
dye [daɪ]	Färbemittel

E

(to) **ease** [iːz]	verringern, erleichtern
economy [ɪˈkɒnəmi]	Wirtschaft
education [ˌedʒuˈkeɪʃn]	Erziehung, Bildung
effect (on) [ɪˈfekt]	(Aus-)Wirkung (auf)
effigy ['efɪdʒi]	Bildnis
effort ['efət]	Mühe, Anstrengung
ejection [ɪˈdʒekʃn]	Vertreibung
elaborate [ɪˈlæbərət]	kunstvoll (gearbeitet); durchdacht
(to) **elect** [ɪˈlekt]	wählen
election [ɪˈlekʃn]	Wahl
emigrant ['emɪgrənt]	Emigrant/in, Auswanderer/in
(to) **emigrate**	emigrieren, auswandern
emigration	Emigration, Auswanderung
employer	Arbeitgeber/in
emulation [ˌemjuˈleɪʃn]	Nacheifern
(to) **enable** sb. **to do** sth. [ɪnˈeɪbl]	es jm. ermöglichen, etw. zu tun
enclosure [ɪnˈkləʊʒə]	Einfriedung, Einzäunung, Einhegung
endowed [ɪnˈdaʊd]	(gut) ausgestattet, gestiftet
(to) **endure** [ɪnˈdʒʊə]	ertragen
(to) **enforce** [ɪnˈfɔːs]	erzwingen
(to) **ensure** [ɪnˈʃɔː]	gewährleisten, garantieren
(to) **entitle** sb. **to do** sth.	jn. berechtigen/jm. das Recht geben, etw. zu tun
entrepreneur [ˌɒntrəprəˈnɜː]	Unternehmer/in
environment [ɪnˈvaɪrənmənt]	Umwelt
epidemic [ˌepɪˈdemɪk]	Epidemie
epigram ['epɪgræm]	Epigramm
(to) **establish**	einführen
establishment [ɪˈstæblɪʃmənt]	Einführung; (Be-)Gründung, Einsetzung
(to) **estimate** ['estɪmeɪt]	(ein-)schätzen
ethnic ['eθnɪk]	ethnisch
~ mix	Völkergemisch
Europe ['jʊərəp]	Europa
European [ˌjʊərəˈpiən]	europäisch
event [ɪˈvent]	Ereignis
eventually [ɪˈventʃʊəli]	schließlich
(to) **exclude** sb. **from** sth. [ɪkˈskluːd]	jn. von etw. ausschließen
executive branch [ɪgˈzekjʊtɪv]	Exekutive, vollziehende Gewalt
(to) **exercise** ['eksəsaɪz]	ausüben
exertion [ɪgˈzɜːʃn]	Anstrengung
exhausted [ɪgˈzɔːstɪd]	erschöpft
exhibition [ˌeksɪˈbɪʃn]	Ausstellung
existence: to come into ~ [ɪgˈzɪstəns]	entstehen
expectation [ˌekspekˈteɪʃn]	Erwartung
expenditure [ɪkˈspendɪtʃə]	Ausgaben
expense [ɪkˈspens]	Kosten
(to) **expire** [ɪkˈspaɪə]	ablaufen, erlöschen
(to) **exploit** [ɪkˈsplɔɪt]	ausbeuten
exploitation [ˌeksplɔɪˈteɪʃn]	Ausbeutung
export(s) ['ekspɔːts]	Export(e), Ausfuhr(en)
(to) **export** [ɪkˈspɔːt]	exportieren, ausführen
eye-witness	Augenzeuge/Augenzeugin

F

(to) **fail**	scheitern, fehlschlagen
(to) **fall**	
~ **to**	fallen auf
~ **by**	fallen um, zurückgehen um
~ **behind**	zurückfallen hinter
~ **out with** sb.	sich mit jm. streiten
fallow land ['fæləʊ]	Brache, Brachland
favourable ['feɪvərəbl]	günstig, positiv
(to) **faze** [feɪz]	verblüffen, überraschen
fear [fɪə]	Angst
federal ['fedərəl]	Bundes-, föderativ
fellow	Kamerad
fertility [fɜːˈtɪləti]	Fruchtbarkeit
(to) **fertilize** ['fɜːtəlaɪz]	düngen
fez	Fes
field [fiːld]	Feld, Acker
(to) **fight**	kämpfen
fighting	Kämpfe
figure ['fɪgə]	Betrag, Zahl, Ziffer
filth [fɪlθ]	Dreck
finally ['faɪnəli]	schließlich, abschließend
fine	Geldstrafe, Bußgeld
finished product	Endprodukt, fertiges Produkt

fit	geeignet, gut, wert(voll)
flag	Flagge
flax	Flachs
flock	Herde, Schwarm
flowing	fließend
fluff [flʌf]	Flusen, Fusseln
(to) follow (from sth.)	(aus etw.) folgen
(to) be ~ed by	als Folge haben
formal ['fɔ:ml]	formell, offiziell
fort	Fort
(to) found	gründen
founder	Gründer/in
foundry ['faʊndri]	Gießerei
fragile ['frædʒaɪl]	zart
frame	Rahmen
franchise ['fræntʃaɪz]	Stimm-/Wahlrecht
fraud [frɔ:d]	Täuschung, Betrug
friendship ['frendʃɪp]	Freundschaft
(to) seek ~ with sb.	freundschaftliche Beziehungen mit jm. anstreben
(to) win sb.'s ~	jemandes Freundschaft gewinnen
from ... till	von ... bis
fuel ['fju:əl]	Brennstoff
fur [fɜ:]	Fell, Pelz
furnace ['fɜ:nɪs]	Ofen

G

(to) gain	gewinnen
gallery ['gæləri]	Galerie
garland ['gɑ:lənd]	Girlande, Kranz
garment ['gɑ:mənt]	Kleidungsstück
(to) gather ['gæðə]	sich versammeln
gear [gɪə]	Gang, Übersetzung
gears	Getriebe
general ['dʒenrəl]	General
generous ['dʒenərəs]	großzügig
German Imperial Eagle [ɪmˌpɪərɪəl_'i:gl]	Deutscher Reichsadler
(to) get on with	auskommen mit
(to) get to	erreichen
giraffe [dʒəˈrɑ:f]	Giraffe
(to) give rise to sth.	etw. verursachen
glamour ['glæmə]	Glanz
(to) glare down [gleə]	(Sonne) herunterbrennen
(to) glitter	funkeln, glänzen
gloomy ['glu:mi]	düster, finster
goods [gʊdz]	Waren
(to) goose-step ['gu:s step]	im Stechschritt marschieren
government ['gʌvənmənt]	Regierung
governor ['gʌvənə]	Gouverneur
grain	Korn, Getreide
grand	grandios, eindrucksvoll
(to) grant [grɑ:nt]	bewilligen
graph [grɑ:f]	Graph
(to) grasp [grɑ:sp]	verstehen
grateful	dankbar
(to) graze	grasen, (ab-)weiden
greedy	geldgierig
grits	Grütze, Haferschrot
grievance ['gri:vns]	Beschwerde, Klage
grog	Grog
ground	
above ~	überirdisch
underground	unterirdisch
(to) grow (by)	wachsen/zunehmen (um)
(to) guard [gɑ:d]	hüten, schützen
guerilla [gəˈrɪlə]	Guerilla

H

habit ['hæbɪt]	Gewohnheit
(to) halt [hɔ:lt]	beenden; anhalten
hammock ['hæmək]	Hängematte
(to) hand over	übergeben/-reichen
harmony ['hɑ:məni]	Harmonie
hatchet ['hætʃɪt]	Beil
headscarf ['hedskɑ:f]	Kopftuch
(to) heat up	erhitzen, heiß machen
height [haɪt]	Größe
helmet ['helmɪt]	Helm
spiked ~	Pickelhaube
helpless	hilflos
heredity [hɪˈredəti]	Vererbung, Erbgut
hide [haɪd]	Haut, Fell
high-capacity pump [ˌhaɪ kəˈpæsəti pʌmp]	Hochleistungspumpe
High Commissioner [ˌhaɪ kəˈmɪʃənə]	Hochkommissar
high society [ˌhaɪ səˈsaɪəti]	vornehme/feine Gesellschaft; obere Gesellschaftsschicht
hippo ['hɪpəʊ]	Nilpferd
(to) hire out	vermieten
hoe [həʊ]	Hacke
(to) hoist [hɔɪst]	aufziehen, hissen, setzen
(to) hold property ['prɒpəti]	Eigentum besitzen
home rule [ˌhəʊm 'ru:l]	Autonomie, Selbstbestimmung
horse power (HP)	Pferdestärke (PS)
householder	Wohnungsinhaber/in
hunger strike	Hungerstreik

I

idyllic [ɪˈdɪlɪk]	idyllisch
(to) ignore [ɪgˈnɔ:]	ignorieren, nicht wissen
(to) illustrate ['ɪləstreɪt]	veranschaulichen, illustrieren
immigrant ['ɪmɪgrənt]	Einwanderer/in, Immigrant/in
(to) immigrate	immigrieren, einwandern
immigration	Immigration
impact ['ɪmpækt]	(Aus-)Wirkung
(to) impel [ɪm'pel]	(an-)treiben
(to) feel ~led to do sth.	sich genötigt/gezwungen fühlen, etw. zu tun
import ['ɪmpɔ:t]	Import, Einfuhr
(to) import [ɪm'pɔ:t]	importieren, einführen
(to) impose [ɪm'pəʊz]	auferlegen, anordnen
imposing	imposant
impressive [ɪm'presɪv]	beeindruckend, imponierend
(to) imprison [ɪm'prɪzn]	einsperren
(to) improve [ɪm'pru:v]	verbessern
improvement	Verbesserung
in	
~ a similar way	auf eine ähnliche Art und Weise
~ a way	auf gewisse Art und Weise, irgendwie
~ bulk	en gros
~ large quantities	in großen Mengen
~ the background	im Hintergrund
~ the family way	(hist.) schwanger
~ the foreground	im Vordergrund
inconvenience [ɪnkən'vi:nɪəns]	Unannehmlichkeit
increase [ɪn'kri:s]	Zunahme, Anstieg
(to) increase [ɪn'kri:s]	stärker/größer werden, zunehmen
independence [ˌɪndɪ'pendəns]	Unabhängigkeit
Declaration of Independence	Unabhängigkeitserklärung

indifference [ɪn'dɪfrəns]	Gleichgültigkeit
indigenous [ɪn'dɪdʒənəs]	einheimisch, eingeboren
indigo ['ɪndɪgəʊ]	Indigo(pflanze)
indivisible [ˌɪndɪ'vɪzəbl]	unteilbar
industrialized [ɪn'dʌstriəlaɪzd]	industrialisiert
inferior [ɪn'fɪəriə]	minderwertig
(to) inflict sth. on sb.	jm. etw. zufügen/versetzen
influence ['ɪnfluəns]	Einfluß
inherent [ɪn'herənt]	innewohnend, natürlich
inlet ['ɪnlet]	Einlaß(ventil)
insane [ɪn'seɪn]	geisteskrank, wahnsinnig
(to) insult sb. [ɪn'sʌlt]	jn. beleidigen
internationalism [ˌɪntə'næʃnəlɪzm]	Internationalismus
intertribal [ˌɪntə'traɪbl]	zwischen verschiedenen Stämmen
(to) invade [ɪn'veɪd]	einmarschieren in
invasion [ɪn'veɪʒn]	Invasion
invention [ɪn'venʃn]	Erfindung
investment [ɪn'vestmənt]	Investition, (Kapital-)Anlage
(to) be involved in	beteiligt sein an
iron ['aɪən]	Eisen
ironware ['aɪənweə]	Eisenwaren
item ['aɪtəm]	Ding, Sache, Artikel
ivory ['aɪvəri]	Elfenbein

J

(to) join	eintreten in; verbinden
joint [dʒɔɪnt]	Gelenk
(to) jolt [dʒəʊlt]	holpern, rütteln, rumpeln
joyful	froh
judicial branch [dʒu'dɪʃl]	Judikative, richterliche Gewalt
jungle ['dʒʌŋgl]	Dschungel
justice ['dʒʌstɪs]	Gerechtigkeit; Richter/in
Justice of Peace	Friedensrichter/in

K

(to) keep cattle	Vieh halten
kind-hearted	gutherzig
(to) knock [nɒk]	schlagen, klopfen
kraal [krɑːl]	Kral

L

label ['leɪbl]	Wäschezeichen
labour ['leɪbə]	Arbeit
child labour	Kinderarbeit
lace [leɪs]	Spitze
(to) lag	zurückbleiben
landlordism ['lændlɔːdɪzəm]	Vermietertum
language	Sprache
native ~	Muttersprache
official ~	Amtssprache
large	
a ~ proportion of ...	ein großer Anteil von
in ~ quantities	in großen Mengen
lately ['leɪtli]	kürzlich, vor kurzem
law [lɔː]	Gesetz
~ enforcement [ɪn'fɔːsmənt]	die Durchsetzung der Gesetze
lbs = pounds	(Gewichtseinheit) Pfund
(to) lead [liːd]	(an-)führen
~ to	führen zu
~ back	zurückführen
leaf, pl. leaves	Blatt
learned ['lɜːnɪd]	gelehrt
legislative branch ['ledʒɪslətɪv]	Legislative, gesetzgebende Gewalt
leisure ['leʒə]	Freizeit
lengthwise ['leŋθwaɪz]	längs angeordnet; der Länge nach
level of the water	Wasserstand
liberty ['lɪbəti]	Freiheit
life: for~	auf Lebenszeit
lion ['laɪən]	Löwe
~'s share	Löwenanteil
literacy ['lɪtrəsi]	Lese- und Schreibfähigkeit
livestock ['laɪvstɒk]	Vieh
(to) load	beladen
loaf, pl. loaves [ləʊf, ləʊvz]	(Brot-)Laib
loan [ləʊn]	Anleihe, Darlehen
lobster	Hummer
location [ləʊ'keɪʃn]	Standort
lodger ['lɒdʒə]	Untermieter/in
(to) loiter ['lɔɪtə]	trödeln, bummeln
(to) look on	zusehen
loom	Webstuhl
lot	Los
(to) lower ['ləʊə]	herab-/hinablassen
Luddite ['lʌdaɪt]	Maschinenstürmer
lyrical ['lɪrɪkl]	lyrisch

M

machinery [mə'ʃiːnəri]	Maschinen, Maschinerie
magnificent [mæg'nɪfɪsnt]	prunkvoll, prächtig
mainspring	Triebfeder
(to) maintain [meɪn'teɪn]	aufrechterhalten
majestic [mə'dʒestɪk]	majestätisch
make-up ['meɪk ʌp]	Zusammensetzung
(to) maltreat [ˌmæl'triːt]	mißhandeln
mandate ['mændeɪt]	Mandat
mangled ['mæŋgld]	verstümmelt
manifestation [ˌmænɪfe'steɪʃn]	Ausdruck
(to) manipulate [mə'nɪpjuleɪt]	manipulieren
manor(-house) ['mænə]	Herrenhaus
(to) manufacture [ˌmænju'fæktʃə]	herstellen
manufacturing	Fabrikation
manure [mə'njʊə]	Dung, Dünger
map	Landkarte
march [mɑːtʃ]	Marsch
massacre ['mæsəkə]	Massaker
meadow ['medəʊ]	Wiese
(to) meet the growing demand	dem steigenden Bedarf begegnen, auf den steigenden Bedarf reagieren
meeting	Treffen
menace ['menəs]	Drohung
(to) mention	erwähnen
mercantilism ['mɜːkəntɪlɪzm]	Merkantilismus
merchant ['mɜːtʃənt]	Kaufmann, Händler/in
merchantman	(hist.) Handelsschiff
(to) merge [mɜːdʒ]	zusammenschließen, zusammenfügen
metropolitan [ˌmetrə'pɒlɪtən]	großstädtisch
midwifery [ˌmɪd'wɪfəri]	Geburtshilfe
(to) migrate [maɪ'greɪt]	auswandern
military ['mɪlətri]	militärisch, Militär-
mill	Mühle
mine [maɪn]	Bergwerk
mine cage ['maɪn keɪdʒ]	(in Bergwerk) Förderkorb
mischief ['mɪstʃɪf]	Unfug
mob	Mob, Pöbel
monkey	Affe
monopoly [mə'nɒpəli]	Monopol
monotonous [mə'nɒtənəs]	eintönig
moreover	und außerdem, zudem

(to) **mortgage** [ˈmɔːgɪdʒ]	verpfänden	**P**	
mother tongue [ˈmʌðə tʌŋ]	Muttersprache		
motion [ˈməʊʃn]	Bewegung	**palm tree** [ˈpɑːm triː]	Palme
The ~ is passed on by ...	Die Bewegung wird weitergeleitet durch ...	(to) **parade** [pəˈreɪd]	marschieren, exerzieren
The ~ is transmitted by ...	Die Bewegung wird durch/von ... übertragen	**parliament** [ˈpɑːləmənt]	Parlament
		part	Teil
motive power [ˈməʊtɪv]	Antriebskraft	**partition** [pɑːˈtɪʃn]	Teilung
motto [ˈmɒtəʊ]	Motto, Wahlspruch	**party**	(pol.) Partei
(to) **multiply** [ˈmʌltɪplaɪ]	vervielfachen, multiplizieren	**pasture** [ˈpɑːstʃə]	Weideland, Futter
musket [ˈmʌskɪt]	Muskete	**pauper** [ˈpɔːpə]	Arme/r, Unterstützungsempfänger/in
mustard seed [ˈmʌstəd]	Senfkorn	~ **children**	Armenhauskinder
mutual [ˈmjuːtʃuəl]	gegenseitig	**paw** [pɔː]	Pfote
		(to) **pay homage to** sb. [ˈhɒmɪdʒ]	jm. huldigen
N		**pea** [piː]	Erbse
naked [ˈneɪkɪd]	nackt	**peaceful**	friedlich
narrow [ˈnærəʊ]	eng	**peak** [piːk]	Gipfel, Höhepunkt
nation [ˈneɪʃn]	Nation	**peanut** [ˈpiːnʌt]	Erdnuß
nationalism [ˈnæʃnəlɪzəm]	Nationalismus	**peasant** [ˈpeznt]	Landarbeiter/in
nationality [ˌnæʃəˈnæləti]	Nationalität, Staatsangehörigkeit	**per year** [pə]	pro Jahr
native [ˈneɪtɪv]	einheimisch, eingeboren; Einheimische/r, Eingeborene/r	**percentage** [pəˈsentɪdʒ]	(prozentualer) Anteil
		peril [ˈperəl]	Gefahr, Untergang
		(to) **perish** [ˈperɪʃ]	umkommen, untergehen
Native Americans	„Indianer"	(to) **permit** sth. [pəˈmɪt]	etw. zulassen, erlauben
navigable [ˈnævɪgəbl]	schiffbar, befahrbar	**petal** [ˈpetl]	Blütenblatt
navigation [ˌnævɪˈgeɪʃn]	Navigation, Navigieren	**petition** [pəˈtɪʃn]	Petition, Eingabe
navy [ˈneɪvi]	Marine	(to) **petition** sb. **for** sth.	jn. um etw. ersuchen
need	Notwendigkeit, Bedarf	**pickaxe** [ˈpɪkæks]	Spitzhacke
the ~ **for** ...	der Bedarf an ...	**pickle**	Salzlake, Marinade
negotiation [nɪˌgəʊʃiˈeɪʃn]	Verhandlung	**pig**	Schwein
neo-classicist [ˌniːəʊˈklæsɪsɪst]	neoklassizistisch	**pigeon** [ˈpɪdʒɪn]	Taube
non-ferrous [ˌnɒn ˈferəs]	Nichteisen-	**Pilgrims** (AE)	Pilgerväter
nostalgic [nɒˈstældʒɪk]	nostalgisch	**pilgrim fathers** (BE)	Pilgerväter
nutrient [ˈnjuːtrɪənt]	Nährstoff	**pillar** [ˈpɪlə]	Pfeiler, Posten
		piston [ˈpɪstən]	Kolben
O		**plantation** [plænˈteɪʃn]	Plantage
		~ **agriculture**	Plantagenwirtschaft
objection [əbˈdʒekʃn]	Einwand, Abneigung	**pledge** [pledʒ]	Gelöbnis, Versprechen
(to) **oblige** [əˈblaɪdʒ]	entgegenkommen	**ploughman** [ˈplaʊmən]	Pflüger
occasion [əˈkeɪʒn]	Anlaß, Gelegenheit	**politician** [ˌpɒlɪˈtɪʃn]	Politiker/in
occupation [ˌɒkjuˈpeɪʃn]	Beruf, Beschäftigung; Besetzung	**politics**	Politik
		(to) **pollute** [pəˈluːt]	verschmutzen, verunreinigen
offering	Gabe	**pollution** [pəˈluːʃn]	(Umwelt-)Verschmutzung
officer	Offizier	**pomp**	Pomp, Prunk
official [əˈfɪʃl]	offiziell, Amts-	**pompous** [ˈpɒmpəs]	pompös, aufgeblasen
oneness [wʌnnɪs]	Einklang, Übereinstimmung	**population**	Bevölkerung
open-minded	aufgeschlossen	~ **growth**	Bevölkerungswachtum
(to) **operate** [ˈɒpəreɪt]	in Betrieb sein; bedienen	**possessions** [pəˈzeʃnz]	Besitz(ungen), Eigentum
opinion	Meinung	**posterity** [pɒˈsterəti]	die Nachwelt
opposition [ˌɒpəˈzɪʃn]	Widerstand	**pound** (1lb=453g, £1=100p)	Pfund
ore [ɔː]	Erz	**prayer book** [preə]	Gebetbuch
(to) **originate from** [əˈrɪdʒɪneɪt]	entstehen aus	**preceding** [prɪˈsiːdɪŋ]	vorige/r, letzte/r
		(to) **prefer**	bevorzugen
outbreak	Ausbruch	(to) **present** [prɪˈzent]	vorlegen, überreichen
outcome	Ergebnis, Resultat	(to) ~ **arms**	die Waffen präsentieren
outlet [ˈaʊtlet]	Auslaßventil	(to) ~ **demands**	Forderungen stellen
output [ˈaʊtpʊt]	Produktion(sertrag); Fördermenge	**president** [ˈprezɪdənt]	Präsident
		pressing board	Preßbalken
(to) **overlay** [ˌəʊvəˈleɪ]	bedecken, überziehen	**pressure** [ˈpreʃə]	Druck
(to) **overtake** [ˌəʊvəˈteɪk]	sich an die Spitze setzen	**prisoner** [ˈprɪznə]	Gefangene/r
(to) **owe** sth. **to** sb. [əʊ]	jm. etw. schulden	(to) **produce** sth. [prəˈdjuːs]	etw. vorlegen; herstellen
(to) **own**	besitzen	**production** [prəˈdʌkʃn]	Produktion, Herstellung
owner	Besitzer/in	**productivity** [ˌprɒdʌkˈtɪvəti]	Produktivität
oz. = ounce [aʊns]	Unze (ca. 0,29 l)	**profit** [ˈprɒfɪt]	Gewinn
		(to) **prohibit** sth. [prəˈhɪbɪt]	etw. verbieten
		prop	Stütze, Strebe
		propaganda [ˌprɒpəˈgændə]	Propaganda
		property [ˈprɒpəti]	Eigentum, Besitz
		~ **qualifications**	Eigentums-/Einkommensnachweis

prosperous ['prɒspərəs]	wohlhabend, erfolgreich	result: as a ~ of	als Folge von
(to) protect [prə'tekt]	beschützen	resurrection [ˌrezə'rekʃn]	Wiederbelebung, Auferstehung
protection	Schutz	(to) retain [rɪ'teɪn]	bewahren, beibehalten
protectionism [prə'tekʃənɪzəm]	Protektionismus	retreat [rɪ'triːt]	Rückzug
protectionist	protektionistisch	(to) retreat	sich zurückziehen, zurückweichen
(to) provide [prə'vaɪd]	besorgen, liefern, bereitstellen	revolution [ˌrevə'luːʃn]	Revolution
(to) provoke [prə'vəʊk]	provozieren, reizen	revolutionary	Revolutionär/in; revolutionär
(to) pull	ziehen	rickets ['rɪkɪts]	Rachitis
(to) ~ a string	einen Faden/eine Kette aufziehen	rifle ['raɪfl]	Gewehr
		rights (pl.)	Rechte
pulley ['pʊli]	Rolle	riot ['raɪət]	Aufruhr, Aufstand, Krawall
(to) pump [pʌmp]	pumpen	(to) rise [raɪz]	steigen
pursuit of happiness [pə'sjuːt]	Streben nach Glück	~ to	aufsteigen zu
		~ by	zunehmen um, steigen um
(to) push (up and down)	(auf und ab) drücken	risky	gefährlich
pyramid ['pɪrəmɪd]	Pyramide	rite [raɪt]	Ritus
		last rites	letzte Ölung
Q		rival ['raɪvl]	Rivale/Rivalin
(to) quadruple ['kwɒdrʊpl]	vervierfachen	rivalry ['raɪvlri]	Rivalität
(to) quarrel (about) ['kwɒrəl]	sich streiten (über)	rod	Stange, Stab
		root	Wurzel
R		rope [rəʊp]	Seil, Tau
(to) raise [reɪz]	(hinauf-)heben	rot	Leberfäule
random: at ~ ['rændəm]	wahllos, willkürlich	rotary motion ['rəʊtəri]	Rotationsbewegung
rascal ['rɑːskl]	Halunke, Schuft	(to) rotate [rəʊ'teɪt]	rotieren, sich drehen; wechseln
rate [reɪt]	Rate, Satz	rotation [rəʊ'teɪʃn]	Rotation, Drehung
raw materials [ˌrɔː mə'tɪəriəlz]	Rohstoffe	crop ~	Fruchtwechsel
(to) reach	erreichen, erzielen	(to) rule	herrschen
(to) react	reagieren	ruler	Herrscher/in
~ by	reagieren mit	rumour ['ruːmə]	Gerücht
~ to	reagieren auf	(to) run	laufen; betreiben
realistic [ˌrɪə'lɪstɪk]	realistisch	rural ['rʊərəl]	ländlich
reason ['riːzn]	Vernunft; Grund	~ worker	Landarbeiter/in
the ~ why ...	der Grund dafür, daß ...	ruthless ['ruːθləs]	rücksichtslos
rebellion	Rebellion, Aufstand		
redress [rɪ'dres]	Entschädigung	**S**	
(to) refer to [rɪ'fɜː]	sich beziehen auf	safety lamp	Sicherheitslampe, Laterne
refuse ['refjuːs]	Abfall	sallow ['sæləʊ]	blaßgelb
regardless of	trotz; ohne Rücksicht auf	(to) salute sb. [sə'luːt]	jn. (förmlich) grüßen
(to) reject [rɪ'dʒekt]	ablehnen	sanitation [ˌsænɪ'teɪʃn]	Hygiene; Kanalisation und Abfallbeseitigung
rein [reɪn]	Zügel		
(to) relate to [rɪ'leɪt]	in Zusammenhang bringen mit	scared: (to) be ~	Angst haben
		scattered ['skætəd]	verstreut, vereinzelt
reliable [rɪ'laɪəbl]	zuverlässig	scheme [skiːm]	Anordnung, Programm, Projekt
(to) relieve [rɪ'liːv]	verringern, abbauen; entlasten	scoundrel ['skaʊndrəl]	Schuft
(to) repeal sth.	(Gesetz, Erlaß usw.) aufheben	scourge [skɜːdʒ]	Geißel
(to) replace (with)	ersetzen (durch)	scramble ['skræmbl]	Gerangel
report [rɪ'pɔːt]	Bericht	scythe [saɪð]	Sense
(to) represent [ˌreprɪ'zent]	verkörpern, darstellen; vertreten	secret ['siːkrət]	geheim
		~ ballot ['bælət]	geheime Wahl
representative	Abgeordnete/r, Vertreter/in	secured [sɪ'kjʊəd]	sicher, gesichert
House of Representatives	Abgeordnetenhaus	seed	Samen(korn), Kern
reproachful [rɪ'prəʊtʃfʊl]	vorwurfsvoll	~ drill	Sämaschine
request [rɪ'kwest]	Bitte, Wunsch	self-confident ['kɒnfɪdənt]	selbstsicher
(to) require	brauchen, benötigen, erfordern	self-evident ['evɪdənt]	offenkundig
		(to) sell	verkaufen
resentment [rɪ'zentmənt]	Groll	(to) ~ products over a wide area	Produkte/Waren über ein weit verstreutes Gebiet verkaufen
resistance [rɪ'zɪstəns]	Widerstand		
resolution [ˌrezə'luːʃn]	Entschließung, Resolution		
resources [rɪ'sɔːsɪz]	Bodenschätze; Ressourcen, Mittel	senate ['senɪt]	Senat
		sentry	Wache
(to) respond (to) [rɪ'spɒnd]	(mündlich oder schriftlich) reagieren (auf)	separation of powers	Gewaltenteilung
		servant ['sɜːvənt]	Diener/in
(to) restrict sb.'s power [rɪ'strɪkt]	jemandes Macht einschränken	(to) settle ['setl]	aushandeln; sich einigen
		(to) ~ a dispute [dɪ'spjuːt]	einen Streit beilegen
restricted	beschränkt		

settlement	Siedlung
settler	Siedler/in
sewage ['suːɪdʒ]	Abwasser
shaft [ʃɑːft]	Schacht
share [ʃeə]	Anteil, Aktie
shearing frame ['ʃɪərɪŋ]	Scherrahmen
sheep [ʃiːp]	Schaf
shield [ʃiːld]	(der) Schild
(to) shrug (one's shoulders)	mit den Achseln zucken
shuttle	Weberschiffchen
silk	Seide
simplification [ˌsɪmplɪfɪ'keɪʃn]	Vereinfachung
simultaneously [ˌsɪml'teɪnɪəsli]	gleichzeitig
sisal ['saɪsl]	Sisalagave
size [saɪz]	Größe
sjambok ['ʃæmbɒk]	Nilpferdpeitsche *(Peitsche aus Tierhaut)*
skill	Geschick, Fertigkeit, Technik
slag [slæg]	Schlacke
slave [sleɪv]	Sklave/Sklavin
~ labour	Sklavenarbeit
slip: ~ of paper	Stück Papier
slogan ['sləʊgən]	Slogan, Schlagwort
smallpox ['smɔːlpɒks]	Pocken
smart	schick, schön
smartly-dressed	vornehm gekleidet
snake	Schlange
snort	Schnauben
socialist ['səʊʃəlɪst]	sozialistisch
~ movement	Arbeiterbewegung
society [sə'saɪəti]	Gesellschaft
solidarity [ˌsɒlɪ'dærəti]	Solidarität
source [sɔːs]	Quelle
sovereignty ['sɒvrənti]	Souveränität, Oberhoheit
(to) sow [səʊ]	(aus-)säen
span [spæn]	(Zeit-)Spanne
over a ~ of ...	über eine (Zeit-)Spanne von ...
(to) sparkle ['spɑːkl]	glitzern, glänzen
spear [spɪə]	Speer
(to) spin	spinnen
spindle	Spindel
spinning wheel	Spinnrad
(to) sponsor ['spɒnsə]	(finanziell) unterstützen
squadron ['skwɒdrən]	Bataillon, Schwadron
squatter ['skwɒtə]	*Siedler/in ohne Rechte auf regierungseigenem Land*
(to) squeeze sth. out of sb.	etw. aus jm. herauspressen
stake	Pfahl
(to) be burnt at the ~	auf dem Scheiterhaufen sterben
stamp distributor [dɪ'strɪbjʊtə]	*Steuerbeamter in den amerikanischen Kolonien*
(to) stand for	bedeuten; symbolisieren
(to) stand in neat rows [rəʊ]	in Reih und Glied stehen
(to) starve [stɑːv]	verhungern
state	Staat
station ['steɪʃn]	*(agrar.)* Farm
statistics *(pl.)* [stə'tɪstɪks]	Statistik
steadily ['stedɪli]	fest, sicher
steam	Dampf
~ enters and exits	Dampf strömt ein und aus
~ power	Dampfkraft, -energie
steep [stiːp]	steil
stem	Stiel, Stamm
stocking	Strumpf
(to) strap	(mit dem Riemen) züchtigen
straw [strɔː]	Stroh
strenuous ['strenjuəs]	anstrengend
strewn: (to) be ~ with [struːn]	übersät sein mit/von
strife [straɪf]	Streit, Zwist
strike [straɪk]	Streik
to be on ~	streiken
to go on ~	in den Streik treten
(to) strike	streiken
(to) strike sb.	jn. schlagen/treffen; jn. beeindrucken, jm. auffallen
strip: ~ of land	Streifen Land
submission [səb'mɪʃn]	Unterwerfung
(to) submit to [səb'mɪt]	sich unterwerfen
succession: in ~ [sək'seʃn]	hintereinander, in Folge
(to) suffer	ertragen; leiden
suffocation [ˌsʌfə'keɪʃn]	Erstickung
(to) suggest (sth. to sb.) [sə'dʒest]	(jm. etw.) vorschlagen
suit [suːt]	Anzug, Kostüm
(to) suit	passen, recht sein
superior [suː'pɪərɪə]	höher, überlegen
superiority [suːˌpɪərɪ'ɒrəti]	Überlegenheit
supersonic [ˌsuːpə'sɒnɪk]	Überschall-
superstition [ˌsuːpə'stɪʃn]	Aberglaube
supervisor ['suːpəvaɪzə]	Aufseher/in
supple ['sʌpl]	geschmeidig
supplies [sə'plaɪz]	Vorräte
supply *(mil.)* [sə'plaɪ]	Nachschub
water ~	Wasserversorgung
(to) supply (sb. with sth.)	(jn. mit etw.) versorgen
(to) support	unterstützen
Supreme Court [suːˌpriːm 'kɔːt]	*Oberster Gerichtshof (der USA)*
(to) surge ahead [sɜːdʒ]	vorpreschen
surgeon ['sɜːdʒən]	Chirurg/in
surgery ['sɜːdʒəri]	Chirurgie
(to) surround	umgeben
survey [sə'veɪ]	Untersuchung
(to) sweep	fegen
(to) symbolize ['sɪmbəlaɪz]	symbolisieren
(to) sympathize (with) ['sɪmpəθaɪz]	Mitleid haben (mit); Verständnis haben (für)

T

(to) take sth. over	etw. besetzen, etw. übernehmen
(to) take the lead	die Führung übernehmen
tap	Hahn
tax	Steuer
(to) tax	besteuern
taxation	Besteuerung
temperance ['temprəns]	Mäßigung, Abstinenz; *(Adj.)* Antialkohol-
tenderness ['tendənəs]	Zärtlichkeit
tension ['tenʃn]	(An-)Spannung
territory ['terətri]	Gebiet, Territorium
theft [θeft]	Diebstahl
thence [ðens]	von dort; von daher
thread [θred]	Faden
threat [θret]	(An-, Be-)Drohung
(to) threaten ['θretn]	(be-)drohen
three-field system	Dreifelderwirtschaft
threefold	dreifach
thrifty ['θrɪfti]	sparsam
thus	dadurch, so
timber	(Bau-)Holz
(to) toil ['tɔɪl]	(hart) arbeiten
toiler	*(pol.)* Kämpfer/in
tool	Werkzeug
top hat	Zylinderhut
trade [treɪd]	Handel
(to) trade	handeln, Handel treiben
training ['treɪnɪŋ]	Ausbildung

(to) tread on [tred]	treten auf	whip	Peitsche
treaty	(Staats-)Vertrag	(to) whip	(aus-)peitschen
trek	(schwierige) Reise, Treck	whistle ['wɪsl]	Pfeife
tremendous [trɪ'mendəs]	gewaltig, enorm	wide	breit
triangular [traɪ'æŋgjələ]	dreieckig, dreiseitig	wimble	(hist.) handbetriebene Bohrmaschine
~ trade	Dreieckshandel		
tribe [traɪb]	Stamm		
(to) trickle	tröpfeln, rinnen	(to) wind [waɪnd]	(auf-)wickeln, spulen
(to) trigger sth. off	etw. auslösen	winding crane ['waɪndɪŋ kreɪn]	Aufzug (in Bergwerk o.ä.)
(to) triple ['trɪpl]	verdreifachen		
troop	Truppe	(to) wipe (down) [waɪp]	(ab-)wischen
turning wheel	Schwungrad	(to) withdraw (from)	(sich) zurückziehen (aus)
turnip ['tɜːnɪp]	Kohlrübe, Steckrübe	witness	Zeuge/Zeugin
turnpike	(historisch) gebührenpflichtige Straße	working	(Bergwerks-)Stollen
		working conditions	Arbeitsbedingungen
twisted	verbogen, verdreht	working hours	Arbeitszeit
twofold	zweifach	worn-out	abgetragen, abgenutzt
		(to) worship ['wɜːʃɪp]	anbeten

U

unalienable [ʌn'eɪliənəbl]	unantastbar
unanimously [juː'nænɪməsli]	einstimmig
unconstitutional [ˌʌnkɒnstɪ'tjuːʃənl]	verfassungswidrig
unitary ['juːnɪtəri]	Zentral-, Einheits-
unity ['juːnəti]	Einigkeit
unpleasant	unangenehm
urban ['ɜːbən]	städtisch
(to) urge [ɜːdʒ]	drängen
urgent ['ɜːdʒənt]	dringend
utopian [juː'təʊpiən]	utopisch

Y

yard [jɑːd]	Yard (= 91cm)
yarn [jɑːn]	Garn
yeoman peasant ['jəʊmən]	Kleinbauer/Kleinbäuerin

Z

zone of influence [zəʊn]	Einflußzone

V

vaccine ['væksiːn]	Impfstoff
valve [vælv]	Ventil
(to) vanish ['vænɪʃ]	verschwinden
vast [vɑːst]	riesig, weit, enorm
vegetation [ˌvedʒɪ'teɪʃn]	Vegetation
veto ['viːtəʊ]	Veto
(to) veto	einlegen
victory ['vɪktəri]	Sieg
victuals ['vɪtlz]	Eßwaren, Proviant
village	Dorf
villager	Dorfbewohner/in
vinegar ['vɪnɪɡə]	Essig
(to) violate ['vaɪəleɪt]	verletzen, verstoßen gegen
violence ['vaɪələns]	Gewalt
vote [vəʊt]	Stimme (bei Wahl)
(to) vote	wählen

W

wage(s) ['weɪdʒ]	(Arbeits-)Lohn
~ rise	Lohnerhöhung
~ reduction	Lohnkürzung, Lohnsenkung
wagon ['wæɡən]	Wagen; Waggon
warfare ['wɔːfeə]	Krieg(sführung)
warrior ['wɒriə]	Krieger/in
wasteland	Ödland, Brachland
waterfall	Wasserfall
weak	schwach
wealth ['welθ]	Reichtum
wealthy	reich
weapon ['wepən]	Waffe
(to) wear out	aufbrauchen, verschleißen
(to) weave	weben
weaving	Weben
weed	Unkraut
wheat [wiːt]	Weizen

Historical dictionary

A

Abfall	refuse
Abfallbeseitigung	sanitation
Abgeordnete/r	Member of Parliament (BE), representative (AE)
Abgrenzung	boundary
ablehnen	(to) reject
Abnahme	decrease
abnehmen	(to) decrease
Abrüstung	disarmament
Agrar-	agrarian
zum Verkauf bestimmtes ~erzeugnis	cash-crop
agrarisch	agrarian
Allegorie	allegory
anbeten	(to) worship
Angaben	data
Angriff	attack
Anspannung	tension
Anteil: prozentualer ~	percentage
Arbeit	labour
arbeiten: hart ~	(to) toil
Arbeitgeber/in	employer
Arbeitsbedingungen	working conditions
Arbeitskraft	labour
Arbeitsplatz	work place
Armee	army
Armenhaus	workhouse
Armenhauskinder	pauper children
Askari	askari
aufgeben	(to) abandon
auflösen	(to) dissolve
aufrechterhalten	(to) maintain
Aufstand	riot
aufziehen	(to) hoist
Augenzeuge/Augenzeugin	eye-witness
ausbeuten	(to) exploit
Ausbeutung	exploitation
Ausfuhr	export
ausführen	(to) export
Ausgaben	expenditure
auslösen: etw. ~	(to) trigger sth. off
Ausstellung	exhibition
Welt~	World Exhibition
auswandern	(to) emigrate
Auswanderer/in	emigrant
Auswanderung	emigration
Auswirkung (auf)	effect (on), impact (on)
Auszubildende/r	apprentice

B

Barbarei	barbarism
Baumwolle	cotton
Baumwollspinnerei	cotton mill
Bedarf	demand
auf den steigenden ~ reagieren	(to) meet the growing demand
Behörden	the authorities
benötigen	(to) require
berechtigen	(to) entitle
Bericht	report
Beruf	occupation
beschäftigen	(to) employ
Beschäftigung	occupation
beschützen	(to) protect
Besetzung	occupation
besiegen	(to) defeat
besitzen	(to) own
Besitzer/in	owner
besteuern	(to) tax
Besteuerung	taxation
bestimmt	determined
Bevölkerung	population
~swachstum	population growth
Bewegung (techn.)	motion
Bewegung (pol.)	movement
Bildung	education
Bittschrift	petition
Bodenschätze	resources
Boden	soil
Boykott	boycott
Brache	fallow land
Bundes-	federal
~regierung	federal government
~staat	federal state
Bürger/in	citizen
Bußgeld	fine

C

Charta	charter
chronologisch	chronological

D

Dauer	duration
Deutscher Reichsadler	German Imperial Eagle
Dienstbote	servant
Dreieckshandel	triangular trade
Dreifelderwirtschaft	three-field system
düngen	(to) fertilize

E

Eigentum	property
Einfluß	influence
~zone	zone of influence
jemandes ~ beschränken	(to) curb sb.'s influence
Einhegung	enclosure
einholen	(to) catch up
Einigkeit	unity
Einwanderer/in	immigrant
einwandern	(to) immigrate
Einwanderung	immigration
einwilligen	(to) consent
Einwilligung	approval
Elfenbein	ivory
Endprodukt	finished product
Entdeckung	discovery
entlassen	(to) dismiss
entschlossen	determined
entstehen (aus)	(to) originate (from)
Entwicklung	development
Epidemie	epidemic
Ereignis	event
Erfindung	invention
erfordern	(to) require
Erklärung der Menschen- und Bürgerrechte	Declaration of the Rights of Man
Erlaubnis	consent
ermöglichen	(to) enable
ernennen	(to) appoint

Ernteertrag	crop	**H**	
ersetzen (durch)	(to) replace (with)	Handel	trade
Erwerb	acquisition	handeln	(to) trade
ethnisch	ethnic	Handelsbilanz	balance of trade
Europa	Europe	Hauptstadt	capital
Europäer/in	European	Helm	helmet
europäisch	European	Herausforderung	challenge
Exekutive	executive branch	Herrenhaus	manor (house)
exerzieren	(to) parade	Herrschaft	chiefdom
Export	export	herrschen	(to) rule
exportieren	(to) export	Herrscher/in	ruler
		herstellen	(to) manufacture
F		hissen	(to) hoist
Fabrikation	manufacturing	Hochkommissar/in	High Commissioner
fallen (um)	(to) fall (by)	Hochleistung	high capacity
fehlschlagen	(to) fail	höher	superior
Feldfrucht	crop	huldigen	(to) pay homage to
Fertigkeit	skill		
Flagge	flag	**I**	
Flußdiagramm	flow chart		
Folge	consequence	Impfstoff	vaccine
als ~ haben	(to) be followed by	Import	import
als ~ von	as a result of	„Indianer"	Native Americans
Forderung	demand	infolgedessen	as a result of
Forderungen stellen	(to) present demands	Investition	investment
Fort	fort		
Freiheit *(pol. u. rel.)*	liberty	**J**	
Freundschaft	friendship		
jemandes ~ gewinnen	(to) win sb.'s friendship	Jahrhundert	century
Friedensrichter/in	Justice of Peace	jährlich	annual
Fruchtwechsel	crop rotation	Jakobinermütze	cap of liberty
Führung	lead *(ohne Pl.)*	je nachdem wie	according to how
die ~ übernehmen	(to) take the lead	Judikative	judicial branch
G		**K**	
Garn	yarn	Kabinett	cabinet
Gebiet	territory	Kanone	cannon
Gefahr	peril	Kapitalanlage	investment
Gefangene/r	prisoner	Karikatur	cartoon
Gegensatz	contrast	Katastrophe	disaster
im ~ stehen	(to) contrast	Kaufmann	merchant
Geldstrafe	fine	Kinderarbeit	child labour
General	general	Kirche	church
Gerangel (um)	scramble (for)	Klee	clover
Gerste	barley	Klima	climate
Geschick	skill	Kohlebergwerk	coal-mine, colliery
Gesetz	law, act of parliament	Kolonialmacht	colonial power
Gesetzesänderung	amendment	Kolonie	colony
gesichert	secured	Kolonist/in	colonist
Gewalt	violence	Kolumne	column
ausführende ~	executive branch	Konflikt	conflict
gesetzgebende ~	legislative branch	Kongreß	congress
gesetzsprechende ~	judicial branch	konkurrieren mit	(to) compete with
Gewaltenteilung	separation of powers	Konsequenz	consequence
Gewinn	profit	kontrastieren	(to) contrast
gleichzeitig	simultaneously	kontrollieren	(to) control
Gouverneur/in	governor	Kosten	expense
Graph	graph	kreuzen: mit dem Schiff ~	(to) cruise
Grausamkeit	barbarism	Krieg	war
Grenze	border, boundary	Krise	crisis
großstädtisch	metropolitan	Kupfer	copper
Grund	reason	kürzen	(to) abridge
gründen	(to) found		
Gründer/in	founder	**L**	
Guerilla	guerilla		
		Landarbeiter/in	rural worker
		Landkarte	map
		ländlich	rural
		Landwirtschaft	agriculture

Laufbahn	career
Legislative	legislative
Lehre	apprenticeship
Lehrling	apprentice
liefern	(to) provide, (to) supply
Lohn	wages
~erhöhung	wage rise, pay rise
~senkung	wage reduction
Löwenanteil	lion's share
Loyalität (gegenüber)	allegiance (to)

M

Marine	navy
marschieren	(to) parade
im Stechschritt ~	(to) goose-step
Maschinenstürmer	Luddite
Massaker	massacre
Meinung	opinion
ihrer/seiner ~ nach	according to her/him
Menge	amount (of)
Merkantilismus	mercantilism
mißhandeln	(to) maltreat
Mittel	resources
Monopol	monopoly
multiplizieren	(to) multiply

N

Nachfrage	demand
nachlassen	(to) decrease
Nachschub	supply
Nährstoff	nutrient
Nation	nation
Nationalismus	nationalism
Naturdünger	manure
Navigation	navigation

O

Oberhoheit	sovereignty
Oberster Gerichtshof	Supreme Court
Offizier	officer
Operation *(med.)*	surgery

P/Q

Parlament	parliament
Partei	party
Pfund	pound (1 lb = 453 gr, 1£ = 100p)
Pickelhaube	spiked helmet
Pilgerväter	pilgrim fathers *(BE)*, Pilgrims *(AE)*
Plantage	plantation
Plantagenwirtschaft	plantation agriculture
Pocken	small pox
Politik	politics
Politiker/in	politician
Pomp	pomp
Präsident/in	president
Produkt	product
fertiges ~	finished product
Produktion(sertrag)	output
Produktivität	productivity
Propaganda	propaganda
Prunk	pomp
Puritaner/in	Puritan
puritanisch	Puritan
Pyramide	pyramid
Quelle	source

R

Rechte	rights
unveräußerliches Recht	unalienable right
Regierung	administration, government
Repräsentantenhaus	House of Representatives
Ressourcen	resources
Revolution	revolution
Revolutionär/in	revolutionary
Rivale/Rivalin	rival
Rivalität	rivalry
Rohstoff(e)	raw material(s)
Rübe	turnip
Rückgang	decrease
Rückzug	retreat

S

Sähmaschine	seed drill
Säulendiagramm	bar chart
Schaubild	diagram
schiffbar	navigable
Schlacht	battle
Schlachtschiff	battleship
Schlagwort	slogan
Schlichtung	arbitration
schließlich	eventually
schmücken	(to) decorate
Schulden	debts
schulden: jm. etw. ~	(to) owe sth. to sb.
Schuldner/in	debtor
Schutz	protection
Senat	Senate
setzen	(to) hoist
sicher	secured
Siedler/in	settler
Siedlung	settlement
Sieg	victory
Sinnbild	allegory
Sklave/Sklavin	slave
Slogan	slogan
Soldat/in	soldier
Souveränität	sovereignty
Spalte	column
Spindel	spindle
spinnen	(to) spin, spun, spun
Spinnerei	spinning mill
Staatenbund	confederation
Staatsstreich	coup d'état
Staat	state, commonwealth
städtisch	urban
Stamm	tribe
zwischen verschiedenen Stämmen	intertribal
Standort	location
stärker/größer werden	(to) increase
Statistik	statistics, a set of statistics
stehen: in Reih und Glied ~	(to) stand in neat rows
Stempelgesetz	Stamp Act
Steuer	tax
Stimmrecht	franchise
Stimme *(bei Wahlen)*	vote
Streben nach Glück	pursuit of happiness
Streit	conflict
symbolisieren	(to) symbolize

T

Technik	skill
Teilung	partition
Treuegelöbnis	pledge of allegiance
Truppen	troops
Tuch	cloth

U

überlegen	superior
umkommen	(to) perish
Umwelt	environment
Unabhängigkeit	independence
Unabhängigkeitserklärung	Declaration of Independence
ungefähr	approximately
Unglück	disaster
Untergang	peril
untergehen	(to) perish
Untersuchung	survey
unterwerfen	(to) submit
Unterwerfung	submission
unterzeichnen	(to) sign
einen Vertrag ~	(to) sign a treaty
Ursache	cause
Ursache-Wirkung	cause-effect relationship

V

Verbesserung	improvement
Verfassung	constitution
Verhandlung	negotiation
verhungern	(to) starve
verlassen	(to) abandon
Vermittlung	arbitration
Vernunft	reason
Versammlung	assembly
Verschmutzung	pollution
versorgen (mit)	(to) supply (with)
verteidigen	(to) defend
Verteilung	distribution
Vertrag	treaty
Vertreibung	ejection
vertreten	(to) represent
Vertreter/in *(einer Gruppe o.ä.)*	delegate
Vertreter/in	representative
verursachen	(to) cause, (to) give rise to
vervielfachen	(to) multiply
vervierfachen	(to) quadruple
Verwaltung	administration
Verzögerung	delay
Veto	veto
~ einlegen	(to) veto
Vieh	livestock
Viehzucht	livestock breeding
vorankommen	(to) advance
Vorfahre/Vorfahrin	ancestor
vorrücken	(to) advance

W

Waffen	arms
die ~ präsentieren	(to) present arms
Wahl	election
geheime ~	secret ballot
wählen	(to) elect, (to) vote for
Wahlkreis	constituency
Wahlrecht	franchise
Wahlspruch	motto
Waren	goods
Wasserversorgung	water supply
weben	(to) weave, wove, woven
Weberschiffchen	shuttle
Webstuhl	loom
Weide	pasture
Weltausstellung	world exhibition
Wettbewerb	competition
Widerstand	resitance, opposition
Wirkung	effect
Wirtschaft	economy

Z

Zeitleiste	time-line
Zeitspanne	time span
Zentralstaat	unitary system
Zeuge/Zeugin	witness
Ziel	aim
Ziel(ort)	destination
zunehmen	(to) increase
zurückgehen um	(to) fall by
zurückziehen: sich ~ aus	(to) withdraw from
Zusammenhang: in ~ bringen mit	(to) relate to
Zusatzartikel *(in Verfassung)*	amendment
zustimmen	(to) consent
Zustimmung	approval, consent
zweifach	twofold

Bildquellen: (s = source)
Archiv für Kunst und Geschichte, Berlin (p. 15, s9; p. 16, s11; p. 23, s2; p. 38, s9; p. 41, s5 (b); p. 45, s17; p. 46, s20, s21; p. 51, s13; p. 52, s18, s21; p59, s44, s45)
Artothek, Peissenberg (p. 6, s5)
The BETTMANN Archive, New York (p. 17, s13; p. 26, s8)
© Bildarchiv Preussischer Kulturbesitz, Berlin, 1995 (p. 6, s7; p. 35, s12; p. 36, s1; p. 44, s12; p. 50, s11; p. 72, s1; p. 73, s3; p. 75, s6; p. 83, s12; p. 84, s1, s2)
The British Library, London (p. 43, s10))
Campbell Soup Company, Camden, New Jersey (p. 2, s1)
Cooperative Union Ltd, Manchester (p. 55, s33)
Deutsches Museum, München (p. 40, s4 (b))
Dornier, Lindau/Bodensee (p. 41, s5 (c))
Das Fotoarchiv, Essen (Henning Christoph) (p. 2, s2)
Foto dpa, Frankfurt (p. 61, s4)
The Fotomas Index, West Wickham, Kent (p. 4, s2; p.19, s4)
© Harenberg Kommunikation, Dortmund 1980, Die bibliophilen Taschenbücher, Propagandapostkarten 1 (p. 80, s8)
The Hulton Deutsch Collection, London (p. 79, s5)
Leeds Development Agency/Leisure Services (p. 28, s1, s2; p. 29, s3)
The Library Company of Philadelphia (p. 3, s4; p. 10, s1; p.18, s1, s2; p.20, s7)
Mansell Collection, London (p. 30, s1; p. 31, s2, s3; p.34, s11; p. 36, s3, s4; p. 38, s8; p. 40, s4 (a); p. 41, s5 (a); p. 42, s9; p. 60, s1)
Mary Evans Picture Library, London (p. 40, s1; p. 42, s8; p. 53, s22, s23; p. 54, s28)
Massachusetts Historical Society, Boston (p. 10, s2; p. 11, s3; p. 12, s6; p. 14, s8)
Mirror Syndication International, London (p. 30, s4; p. 49, s5, s8)
National Museum of Labour History, Manchester (p. 55, s32; p. 57, s39, s40)
National Railway Museum, York (p. 39, s11)
Panos Pictures, London (p. 77, s13)
Plimoth Plantation, Plymouth, MA (p. 4, s3)
Henrik Pohl, Berlin (p. 3, s5)
Punch Publications Ltd, London (p. 39, s12; p. 60, s3; p. 67, s6; p. 68, s1)
Rover Group, Birmingham (p. 61, s5)
Rural History Centre, University of Reading, Reading (p. 35, s13)
Copyright 1987,1991 TIME Inc. New York. Reprinted by permission. (p. 23, s3; p. 27, s1)
Tropix Photographic Library (J. Lines), Wirral, Merseyside (p. 85, s5)
F. Zecchin/Magnum/FOCUS, Hamburg (p. 74, s5)
Zinser Textilmaschinen GmbH, Ebersbach/Fils (p. 40, s4 (c))

Textrechte: The State of the Art, Orbit Books 1993, © Iain M. Banks, 1991, London (p. 61, s6); CHRAIBI Driss: La Civilisation, ma mère! © by Editions Denoël, Paris (p. 74, s4)

Nicht alle Copyrightinhaber konnten ermittelt werden; deren Urheberrechte werden hiermit vorsorglich und ausdrücklich anerkannt.